Bro Eli B.

It's a pleasure

Thank God f.

I pray He blesses you and the family

Bro Ellard Thomas

9/24/15

Defeating Goliath

Ellard Thomas, MBA

WestBow Press books may be ordered through booksellers or by contacting:

WestBow Press
A Division of Thomas Nelson & Zondervan
1663 Liberty Drive
Bloomington, IN 47403
www.westbowpress.com
1 (866) 928-1240

ISBN: 978-1-5127-0631-4 (sc)
ISBN: 978-1-5127-0633-8 (hc)
ISBN: 978-1-5127-0632-1 (e)

Library of Congress Control Number: 2015912642

Print information available on the last page.

WestBow Press rev. date: 8/13/2015

Contents

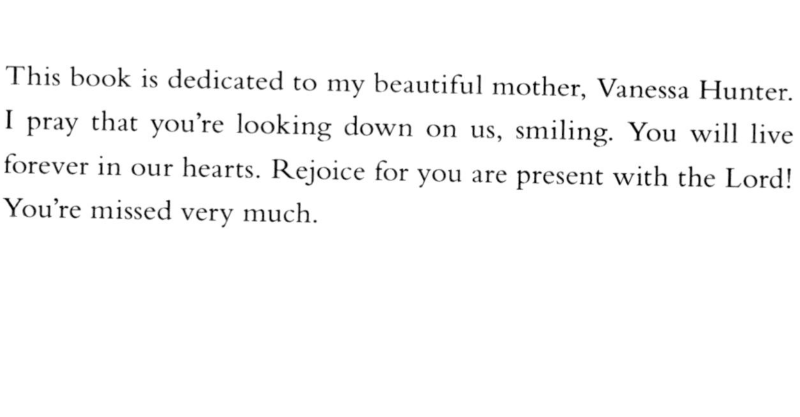

This book is dedicated to my beautiful mother, Vanessa Hunter. I pray that you're looking down on us, smiling. You will live forever in our hearts. Rejoice for you are present with the Lord! You're missed very much.

Foreword

I know something about you. You are one step away from one of your biggest victories. There is an almost insurmountable obstacle in your way, but unlike everyone around you, you believe in your ability to defeat it. You are a modern-day David in front of your own personal Goliath. Perhaps this book is one of your five stones. Or maybe it is your newfound resolve to defeat the giant in front of you with the tried weapons of past battles you thought were insignificant. Whatever the cause of you picking up this book, your decision to defeat Goliath is one, like David, that propels you from where you were yesterday, to a future of relentless pursuit beyond today's good, so that you can embrace tomorrow's best.

Ellard Thomas calls the information in his book, "Goliath-slaying principles." Principles are comprehensive, they are fundamental, and they are guidelines for those that follow them. If you were afraid of your "Goliath" in the past, or refused to face this "Goliath," I submit to you that your principles developed a belief that hindered your victory. With this set of guideposts, you can now move forward to slay what looked like a giant in your life.

Over the past year, I have developed a resolve that struggle will come in my life as a consequence of living. Throughout life there is the pain of changes that we go through. Whether this pain is from a voluntary change like a new career path, or an involuntary pain like the death of a loved one, we must realize that struggles come to us, and often at the most inopportune times. What resolve do we have when such challenges occur? Will we simply cower like the children of Israel at the intimidating presence of painful experiences? Or will we have the courage in us to face new challenges head on? Like David, this choice is ours, and our willingness to engage in the fight is the first step.

Early in my life, I began reading through the Bible with a study of David. We know David by this story that "put him on the map." Perhaps we do not know that David's success in defeating Goliath was not haphazard, accidental, or "lucky." David was a skilled warrior by his own admission. His battles were not confined or limited to the battlefield. You in turn may not see yourself as a warrior, but if you have ever had to fight mentally, emotionally, financially, or with your health, you are a warrior. In those battles for your mind, your peace, your finances, or any other part of your wellbeing, there were probably some obstacles you were against. This is the beauty of your story. There is a little David in us all in a face-off with our own personal Goliath.

Israel in the time of its encounter with the Philistines during the reign of King Saul had limited weapons. The ironsmiths used by Israel were outsourced from Philistia. When war was inevitable, these ironsmiths refused to serve the Israelites. Standing around the valley of Elah, Israel and Philistia gathered. The Philistines taunted the Israelites with their champion, an almost ten-foot, seasoned warrior who challenged Israel to battle, basically with inadequate weapons. This is where David's story speaks to us. As Thomas writes, it is the "foundation of underdog" stories.

We love David's story for its lopsided odds against the champion of the story and the courage and fortitude of the victor. But, lest we distance ourselves from being victorious, remember that we too have the same ability to apply the principles that David did. I believe that it is the principles that brought you to this book. Because I know something about you. Your Goliath, whatever it may be, cannot overcome you. You are and have always been greater than your biggest challenge.

You are a champion! You have everything you need to defeat Goliath! Your victory awaits you!

Dr. Erick G. Pryor

Introduction

An individual to whom God has given purpose, vision or a dream will inevitably meet challenges. Some of these may appear insurmountable while others disabling. Despite how difficult or complex they may seem, however, God desires you victorious.

You may ask, "*How is victory possible when opposition overwhelms me?*" "*How do I enter my destiny when trials greet me at every turn*?"

God created you as a fearfully and wonderfully made individual. Embedded within your sophisticated design of intelligence, adaptability and understanding lays an unstoppable force. This intrinsic force has the power to help you surmount obstacles, to break chains of generational curses and to end feelings of inadequacy, insignificance and insecurity. Furthermore, this explosive force will cause you to elevate higher than you ever thought imaginable. The epic and legendary battle between David and Goliath unveils the type of power deeply seeded within you.

> During the reign of King Saul, Israel had been in constant battle with the Philistines—a fierce and vicious people standing as obstructions to Israel's destiny. Heavily engaged in battle, the king and his men would face

> a warrior never before encountered in warfare: the undefeated giant, Goliath.
>
> Goliath was not any regular warrior. Standing over nine feet tall, wearing almost 200 pounds of armor with complementing weaponry, Goliath was not the average Philistine. Intimidatingly massive, and with an appetite for destruction, he invoked the spirit of fear in the king and his men, thus hindering their progress.
>
> For forty days, Goliath provoked and taunted the men of Israel to fight. Neither Saul nor his men accepted the death-match invitational. The king's faith withered. The men grew restless with concern. Victory faded far into the distance.
>
> While fear continued to grip the king and his men, God intervened. Rather than wipe out Israel's greatest enemy, He sent a young, unknown shepherd boy named David. By the hands of this fearless youngster, Goliath would astonishingly meet his demise. David's courageous action restored the king's faith and returned strength in his men.
>
> –1 Samuel 17

The epic story of David's victory over Goliath stands as the foundation of all underdog stories. It reveals how perceivably unwinnable battles could result in victory by unknown, underestimated and uncommon people. Although a great tale, you may ask, "How does this story about David relate to me?"

David is more than a giant-killing character enlivened by theology or scripture. He's a direct representation of the "force" deeply seeded within you. He's the part of you whom God summons when no one else has the courage to stand up and fight giants. He's your warrior with the power to destroy the image of impossibility.

In the presence of unbearable opposition, your "David" has the power to crush any giant standing between you and your success; between you and your happiness; between you and your deliverance; between you and your financial stability; and between you and your purpose. At your conception, God breathed these giant-defeating attributes into you: relentlessness, resilience, power and unwavering courage. Everything you would ever need to become successful, happy and empowered lies deep within you.

Regardless of the adverse situations you face, or the ill feelings you have experienced from others, it's important for you to understand these subsequent sentences. You will prevail over opposition! You will overcome adversity! You will conquer addictions! You will achieve success! You will operate in the purpose for which you are called! You will destroy generational curses! You will recover from heartache! You will achieve your destiny! You will recover and heal from loss! You will change the way people see you! Through your David, you will achieve greatness!

One

Identify Your Goliath

And the Philistines stood on a mountain on the one side, and Israel stood on a mountain on the other side: and there was a valley between them. And there went out a champion out of the camp of the Philistines, named Goliath, of Gath, whose height was *six cubits and a span* [approximately nine feet nine inches]. And he had a helmet of brass upon his head, and he was armed with a *coat of mail* [metal plates]; and the weight of the coat was *five thousand shekels* of brass [approximately 167 pounds]. And he had *greaves of brass upon his legs* [leg armor], and a *target of brass* [chest plate] between his shoulders. And the staff of his spear was like a weaver's beam; and his spear's head weighed six hundred shekels of iron: and one bearing a shield went before him.

–1 Samuel 17:4-7 KJV, emphasis added

Your future holds immeasurable value. Whatever God has dropped into your spirit to achieve, He means for it to happen.

Success? Yes.

Love? Yes.

Healing? Yes.

Deliverance? Yes.

Purpose? Yes.

Vision? Yes.

Greatness? Yes.

God desires these blessings for your life, but rarely are they easily achieved. God has them mysteriously incubated in challenges and hardships. This raises the question, "Why would God gift wrap my future in adversity?" There are three reasons:

1. Affliction provokes you to face obstacles squarely.
2. Adversity gives birth to fortitude.
3. Adverse circumstances cultivate creativity.

If this is the case, what is God telling us?

God does not want us to be fearful or worried about our situations. He instead wants us to envision them as He sees them—as *opportunities.* Where we see unconquerable challenges, God sees opportunity. Where we see insurmountable obstacles, God sees opportunity. Where we see danger, God sees opportunity. Where we see sadness, God sees opportunity.

What are these opportunities that we should expect? To become great, to break the chains of mediocrity, to turn hopelessness into hopefulness, to turn faithlessness into faithfulness, to turn unhappiness into happiness, and to see the true meaning of GOLIATH: **G**od's **O**pportunity **L**ies **I**n **A**dversity, **T**rials, and **H**indrances.

The Characteristics of Goliath

Understand your enemy's nature and his ways; only then can you expose his weakness!

—Ellard Thomas

Gaining victory over the giants in your life requires you to identify and understand their nature. Examination of Goliath, for example, reveals three attributes of this infamous warrior.

1. The title of champion suggests he had never been defeated. Since he had never lost a battle, the Philistines gained confidence through his reputation and his accomplishments (1 Samuel 17:4).
2. Goliath's appearance provoked intimidation. Standing over nine feet tall, heavily covered in armor and weaponry, his freakish size caused Israel to abandon hope and to relinquish their faith. Individuals gripped by intimidation will ultimately lose clarity about their God-given abilities and thus operate out of a spirit of fear (1 Samuel 17:5-7).
3. Goliath's antagonistic and arrogant demeanor further exposed Israel's cowardice. Standing before the men of Israel, he presented an attractive yet discouraging proposal. If the elect of Israel could defeat him, the Philistines would become enslaved to King Saul and Israel. If, however, the elect of Israel were defeated, Israel would become enslaved to the Philistines (1 Samuel 17:8-9).

As Goliath was to King Saul and his men, your opposition wants to stop your progress and snatch your desire for achievement. It wants to rob you of hope and push you to abandon your faith. That said, what about Goliath caused Israel's fear and reluctance to fight? Was it his size? No. His undefeated track record? No. His antagonistic, arrogant behavior? No.

A much larger, invisible issue caused Israel's dismay and fear: misperception. The men perceived Goliath as invincible and more powerful and stronger than them. Unfortunately, this misperception, or delusion, exposed their lack of faith and misidentification of their enemy.

When dominated by the sight of opposition, you negate the power God has poured into you. You discredit your Creator whenever you place greater faith in your inability rather than His ability within you. This is unacceptable and can no longer continue!

During your moments of weakness or most difficult times, God is your source of power (2 Corinthians 12:9). He is your refuge, strength and a very present help in the time of trouble (Psalms 46:1). Important to understand, He can do whatever you cannot. And since "God did not give us the spirit of fear, but of power, love and a sound mind" and the strength "to tread on serpents and scorpions and over all the power of the enemy," you should never bow down to your challenges (2 Timothy 1:7[KJV]).

Before you think about fleeing from hardship, consider whose image in which you were created: God's. As an individual created in His likeness, you have dominion over every obstacle and issue that has become a Goliath in your life (Genesis 1:26; Luke 10:19). Intimidation then is not part of your God-netic makeup.

Who or What Is Your Giant?

For we do not wrestle against flesh and blood, but against principalities, against powers, against the rulers of the darkness of this age, against spiritual hosts of wickedness in the heavenly places!

—Ephesians 6:12^NKJV^

Progressing successfully in purpose requires you to identify your giant. Whereas Goliath stood as a monstrosity to Israel's success, he represents in your life any person or situation that stands between you and your destiny, reflecting challenges that snag your advancement. Disempowering family members, negative-speaking friends, stagnated relationships, self-defeating thoughts, broken heartedness, and unproductive activities are all examples of giants that may have delayed, detoured, demoralized, or impeded your achievement.

Many of us are oblivious to our giants. We often find solace in the darkness of ignorance and comfort in the warmth of denial. The following questions may help reveal who or what hinders you from operating in purpose, acquiring happiness, and achieving success:

- Who or what presently opposes my chances at higher achievement and happiness?
- Who or what has caused me to give up on my purpose or vision?
- Where and with whom do I spend most of my time when I should be working on my future?

In answering these questions, you may find that your giant falls within the Top Seven Goliaths to Destiny.

1. Unforgiveness
2. Heartache
3. Fear
4. Misfortune
5. Your Past
6. Self
7. Addiction

The Top Seven Goliaths to Destiny have forced many people to quit on their dreams, abandon hope, lose faith, relinquish opportunities to others, and live life without purpose. Countless people have become victimized either by one, a few, or all of these monsters. If you are not operating in the life God called you to live, identify which of these Goliaths is your present giant.

The Goliath of Unforgiveness

Get rid of all bitterness, rage and anger, brawling and slander, along with every form of malice. Be kind and compassionate to one another, forgiving each other, just as in Christ God forgave you.

—Ephesians 4:31-32[NIV]

The Goliath of Unforgiveness has hindered many people from entering into a state of happiness. It has destroyed homes, severed relationships, and led many down the path of hopelessness. As a result, these individuals rarely experience joy in relationships, as distrust becomes the foundation of their connections. They sadly find themselves making the following statements:

- "Why forgive the people who have hurt me when they do not deserve it?"
- "If I forgive them, doesn't that mean they got away with it?"
- "I'd rather hate them than give them the satisfaction of *my* forgiveness."

Sound familiar?

Not forgiving someone who had hurt you is understandable, perhaps even justifiable. Seldom is it the solution to a promising future. Peter's conversation with Jesus serves as a good example.

Presumably afflicted, Peter asks how many times an individual should forgive another. Seven times? For many of us, forgiving someone seven times is more than enough. Knowing Peter's heart, Jesus responds, "I do not say to you, up to seven times, but up to seventy times seven" (Matthew 12:21–22[KJV]). Considerably more than Peter had initially thought.

Forgiving the culprits of your hurt may feel detestable. You are not alone in this feeling. A large majority feels the same way. Why does the thought of forgiveness cause such intense disgust?

Forgiveness is a spiritual design. It requires us to bypass our natural feelings and to tap into the power of our spiritual selves. Unfortunately, this action creates internal conflict, as the natural self often opposes the spiritual persona (Galatians 5:17).

When Jesus stated seventy times seven, many would conclude 490 times as the amount to forgive someone. This was not the

Lord's intent. Rather, He wants us to have a deeper understanding about forgiveness.

God has forgiven us for the hurts we have caused to others, knowingly and unknowingly. Therefore, we ought to forgive others as well. He has forgiven us of our errors, and we should follow His example. And since we "all have sinned and fall short of the Glory of God," He harbors no angst against us. Why then should we against others? (Romans 3:23[KJV]).

In Matthew 18, Jesus speaks a parable about a man who struggles with forgiveness and reveals his unfortunate outcome.

> Therefore, the kingdom of heaven is like a king who wanted to settle accounts with his servants. As he began the settlement, a man who owed him ten thousand talents was brought to him. Since he was not able to pay, the master ordered that he and his wife and his children and all that he had be sold to repay the debt. The servant fell on his knees before him. "Be patient with me," he begged, "and I will pay back everything." The servant's master took pity on him, canceled the debt and let him go. But when that servant went out, he found one of his fellow servants who owed him a hundred denarii. He grabbed him and began to choke him. "Pay back what you owe me!" he demanded. His fellow servant fell to his knees and begged him, "Be patient with me, and I will pay you back." But he refused. Instead, he went off and had the man thrown into prison until he could pay the debt.

> When the other servants saw what had happened, they were greatly distressed and went and told their master everything that had happened. Then the master called the servant in. "You wicked servant," he said, "I canceled all that debt of yours because you begged me to. Shouldn't you have had mercy on your fellow servant just as I had on you?" In anger his master turned him over to the jailers to be tortured, until he should pay back all he owed. This is how my heavenly Father will treat each of you unless you forgive your brother from your heart.
>
> –Matthew 18:21-35[NKJV]

The parable exposes the strength of unforgiveness. If left unaddressed its power can turn potentially great people into careless, emotional wrecks.

Until I Forgave

As a child I underwent years of sexual, emotional and physical abuse. When I sought help no one believed me. I was called a liar and troublemaker. Realizing that I had no voice, I no longer fought my abusers. Instead, I embraced the mistreatment—the beatings—the molestations—the degrading remarks—until I became numb and filled with hate.

Once I entered adulthood, I brought my unquenchable hatred from years past with me. I broke the heart of every woman who loved me. I shattered friendships over

> foolish debates. Whomever disagreed with me had to leave my life. I needed no one! Often finding myself alone I realized the untruth of such a thought. I do need people. I want a relationship. But how? How do I break free from the person who was manufactured and conditioned by a ruthless environment? How can I ever trust anyone again? How do I find the strength to love anyone, including myself?
>
> After years in search of an answer, I found it: forgiveness. I didn't want to forgive those who hurt me. More desirably, I no longer wanted to hurt anyone else. Once I embraced forgiveness and forgave those who hurt me (as well as forgive myself), I lived happier and healthier. I found love and built incredible relationships. The scars from my past are still there, but the wounds are finally healed. I could've saved years of anguish if I had learned about forgiveness a decade ago.

Are you holding grudges? Have you been hurt by a loved one or by a friend? Your decision not to forgive will obstruct your path to ultimate happiness. God is ready to bless you with meaningful relationships and emotional freedom, but you must overcome unforgiveness. Forgive your abusers, hurters, attackers or betrayers so you can live a happier life.

Unforgiveness has no value in the quality of life. The resentment, hostility, hatred or anger you have for your transgressor blocks your blessings. Yes, it's difficult to forgive someone who left you scarred emotionally, physically or financially. Yes, it is hard not to take revenge on those whom hurt you as they seem to live without consequence. Countless people feel as you do. Yet, as a believer you're required by God to forgive them. The doors of your destiny can only swing open after you defeat unforgiveness.

No matter how cruel the actions by others, or how disrespectful their words, you must strive to forgive them. Although difficult you must remember this point: Forgiveness isn't for them; it's for you. It's to set you free, and to allow you the happiness you deserve.

The Goliath of Heartache

Forget the former things; do not dwell on the past. See I am doing a new thing! Now it springs up; do you not perceive it? I am making a way in the wilderness and streams in the wasteland.

–Isaiah 43:18-21NIV

God never intended for you to be alone. He desires you to share your life with another. In Genesis 2:18NIV, God says, "It's not good for the man to be alone. I will make a helper suitable for him."

Unfortunately, we often choose mates based on emotional voids and physical attraction rather than consult God for His direction. Relationships based on attraction or emotions absent purpose usually lead to heartache. If you ever experienced a divorce or had a relationship go awry, you're aware of the devastation heartache leaves behind.

If not properly managed, heartache will become an obstruction to your future. Under the duress of this pain, we often lose zeal for living, make promises not to love again, or confine ourselves to loneliness. We convince ourselves that these activities will "protect" us from others. This is not living life.

Whereas many people will become a hermit following heartache, some of us have a desire to get past our hurt. Sadly, no matter how hard we try, moving forward seems impossible. Why is breaking the cycle of heartache such a difficult task?

Investing time, love, energy, trust and resources into someone creates an intimate bond of honesty and respect. The longer the relationship tie, the stronger the bond becomes. Once the bond is broken either by dejection, betrayal, untruthfulness, deceitfulness, unacceptable behaviors, or unreciprocated feelings, the hurt individual usually becomes vulnerable to vengeful, irrational and illogical thoughts and feelings.

If you have ever experienced heartache due to divorce or relational failure, for example, you know firsthand the crippling feelings that follow: anger, disappointment, frustration, resentment and vengefulness. If left unresolved, these emotions will lead you down a path of destruction or provoke you into irreversible actions. Although you may want to avenge your heart, or seek ways to recoup your losses, spend this time and energy productively. Operate in God's purpose or vision for your life. One may ask, "How do I let go and move forward when I've been trampled on and mistreated?"

Rather than hate the man who shattered your heart, consider the lessons he taught you. Make a list of the positive ways that she has contributed to your life. Take a moment to set aside your emotions and ask, "*What did I like about this person, and what will I never tolerate again*?" Whether positive or negative, relationships teach us a little more about ourselves. They make us define who is better suited for our lives based on purpose, not necessarily on emotions alone. Romans 8:18[NIV] promotes, "I consider that our present sufferings [hurt, disappointment, anguish] are not worth comparing with the glory that will be revealed in us."

You are too attractive and have too much value. Do not spend another moment weeping over someone who has abandoned the relationship or marriage. Let him go! Set her free! Their purpose in your life is over and new opportunities abound. God had to move your "ex" so He can bring you to your "next." Besides, a diamond in the hands of a fool is merely a shiny rock. Yet, that same diamond in the hands of a jeweler is a rare, valuable and precious stone. Such an individual knows how to treat something of great worth. Let God put you in the hands of someone who knows and appreciates your value!

The Goliath of Fear

Be strong and of good courage, do not fear nor be afraid of them; for the LORD your God, He is the One who goes with you. He will not leave you nor forsake you.

–Deuteronomy. 31:6[NKJV]

Fear is a beautifully crafted weapon. It's designed specifically to destroy your dreams, desires and goals. As with any powerful weapon, it has slain, and continues to slay, millions with the potential for greatness. In your pursuit of something greater, you may have experienced the havoc of fear in your own life. It may have stopped you from acting on resounding, world-changing ideas. It may have forced you to forfeit purpose, prosperity and happiness. It may have pushed you to shelve your desires and dreams.

Too often we let fear direct our paths. Too often we sit on the balconies of "what if" as we look down at those more courageous than we. Although God gives us great plans for success, or grants us the desires of our heart, we let fear create doubt in our minds.

> "Go after your dreams," God says, but fear whispers, "what if you fail?"
>
> "Operate in your purpose," God says, but fear says, "no one will support you."
>
> "Have faith in the ability I gave you," God says, but fear utters, "If you don't succeed, what will your friends and family say about you?"

Many debates have occurred to determine whether fear motivates or prohibits people from reaching the summit of their potential. The debates are extensive. Some writers go as far to say that a "healthy" fear of something is plausible, normal even. Unless that "something" is God, fear seldom has healthy attributes. It often promotes worry, overwhelming concern and deters people from using their God-given gifts.

Nationally acclaimed actor (and widely admired entertainer) Will Smith recited something phenomenal in the movie After Earth. Playing the role of a confident, disciplined and highly revered military officer Smith said:

> "Fear is not real. The only place that fear can exist is in our thoughts of the future. It is a product of our imagination, causing us to fear things that do not at present and may not ever exist. That is near insanity. Do not misunderstand me, danger is very real, but fear is a choice."
>
> –After Earth, 2013

There's something you must know about fear. It does not have power unless you give power over to it. This happens when you accept it in your life. This acceptance often occurs through the sight of, or at the introduction to, new opportunities or new challenges. Disqualifying yourself as the "right" person for a particular job, for example, often stem from fear. Regardless of the situations, hardships, or obstacles you face, you are the right person. You are far more capable than anyone else to fulfill the vision or opportunity before you. If you were not the right one, God would not have chosen you.

In the Book of Numbers, scripture reveals how fear cost a nation an incredible future. Consider your own life as you read this.

> God tells Moses to send some men to survey Canaan (The Promise Land) to see the type of land that He desired to give the people of Israel. Compliant to God's direction, Moses sends twelve men—one person from each tribe—and advises them to bring back "some of the fruit of the land" as evidence for the people (Numbers 13:17).
>
> Upon spying out the land as commanded, the twelve return with a sampling of grapes and pomegranates.

> The land truly flowed "with milk and honey," a phrase synonymous to prosperity and opportunity.
>
> Although the people see a portion of their future, the majority of the men talk about the strength and size of the country's inhabitants. Looking at each other, they conclude themselves weaker and smaller than they. Interestingly, Moses neither requests information about the country's occupants nor the men's feelings of inadequacy. Driven by fear the men thought it necessary to give it (Numbers 13: 21-28).

The people of Israel had become an obstruction to their own destiny. Turning their attention towards their obstacles rather than on their blessings ruined a blissful life. Everything they desired awaited them, but they were robbed by fear.

As mentioned earlier, fear has only the power you give it. Your emotional investment and time strengthen its foothold. If you have ever encountered fear, or it currently runs rampantly in your life, read the following statement carefully: "**If you ever hope to achieve the blessings of God, you must determine how long you're willing to let fear control you**." It's time to take back your life!

If you're tired of being afraid, look fear in its face and say, "I am greater than you." Stare at it and yell, "I will not let you stop me from getting all God has for me!" Tell it, "I am breaking free from you today!"

Despite all you may undergo, do not let fear hinder you any longer! Decide today to go after the promises of God with everything you got! Right now is your time. Say these words aloud: "Right now is my time!"

The Goliath of Misfortune

When you pass through the waters, I will be with you; and through the rivers, they shall not overflow [overtake] you. When you walk through the fire, you shall not be burned, nor shall the flame scorch you.

– Isaiah 43:2^{NKJV}, emphasis added

Financial loss. Death. Illness. Misfortune. Life's mysterious and unexplainable travesties discriminate against no one. Without notice, they shake our foundation of stability and rattle our belief systems. Following the turmoil, we're left to find balance on the rocky floors of uncertainty, clarity in the dust of confusion and encouragement in the crevice of anguish. Stricken with grief, we often become unmotivated. The pursuit of vision or purpose then slowly fades away.

Misfortune is another Goliath. Due to this giant dreams fail to manifest, ideas never implemented, and goals never achieved. As a result, a great number of people leave this world without fulfilling their purpose. This will not be you! Yet, if you hope to slay misfortune, you first must understand what it is.

What is Misfortune?

Misfortune is, "an unfortunate condition or event." Perhaps a more suitable definition is, "any event or circumstance which hinders purpose, holds up progress and impedes advancement." Moreover, it's the tragic events, losses and perceivably insurmountable hardships that make living unbearable.

The Birth of Misfortune

Have you ever asked from where does misfortune come? Most people are unaware of its birth or inception. Misfortune either comes from God to provoke greater in us, or it's used by demonic forces to sway us from having faith. Strangely, during adverse circumstances, it's difficult to determine who the initiator of our misfortune is: *God* or *Satan*?

God often uses misfortune as a method to strengthen or to bless you. He uses it to help jumpstart your destiny. God knows that many people will not pursue purpose unless a shift happens.

Satan, however, uses misfortune to kill your vision, contaminate your spirit and keep you bound. He does this because he understands a very important fact: destroying your faith in God will stop you from achieving destiny. If he can tip the scales in his favor, Satan hopes to draw you away from God—your ultimate source of power. He tried this same tactic on Job.

In the Book of Job, God allows Satan to bring misfortune into Job's life. One would think God ruthless, or without regard for Job's life, to let Satan run amuck, right? Contrarily, God loved and favored Job. He had a great relationship with him. God simply wanted to make Satan aware of Job's unbreakable integrity. God wanted him to understand that Job's relationship with Him stemmed beyond worldly possessions.

Job had it all: a relationship and favor with God, wealth, a loving family, and servants. He lived the life many people desired. Unfortunately, Job would experience a chain of life-changing, painful events.

As God and His sons conversed with one another, Satan approached them. Upon Satan's arrival, God asked, "from where have you come?" Satan answered, "From going to and fro the earth, and walking back and forth on it."

God knowing Satan's lust for destruction then asked, "Have you considered my servant Job, that there is none like him on the earth, a blameless and upright man, one who fears God and shuns [hates] evil?"

Considering God's question, Satan reminds God about the hedge, or protective barrier, He built around Job, his household and everything connected to him. After itemizing all God had given Job, Satan further tells Him that Job will turn his back, or lose faith, if he were to lose everything.

Knowing Job's character, <u>God gives Satan power</u> to do as he pleases, but with one stipulation. Satan couldn't take Job's life. Upon agreeing to the rules, Satan initiates several attacks, urging Job to turn his back on God.

The level of attacks Job experiences would break most men. Satan takes Job's wealth and the lives of his children.

> He covers Job with painful boils (sores). Following these attacks, Job's wife encourages him to curse God and die. And rather than provide comfort, Job's friends visit only to taunt and judge him.
>
> – Book of Job

How much pain must one endure before quitting? How much loss is enough? Everything Job worked for, and built, diminished. Imagine the emotional pain and pressure these attacks put on his marriage. Think about the amount of grief he carried. The negative emotions he felt. Perhaps you can relate.

Satan's acts were designed to break Job's relationship with, and trust in, God. He failed miserably. Despite his hurt and losses, Job kept his integrity and his character intact. During his darkest moments he continued to trust God. Job's commitment during misfortune reveals a path we all should follow: trust God regardless of our emotions. Once Job passed the "test" God blessed him with more than he had before (Job 42:12).

Your misfortune is God's setup to greater blessings. Surely, you may want to give up as you think about your losses or adverse circumstances, but keep this in mind: <u>God will bring you through it</u>. Trust Him when hope diminishes. Trust Him when disaster strikes. Trust Him when friends and family speak profanely against you. Trust Him because He will never leave you nor forsake you.

Despite the losses or hurt you've undergone, or are presently undergoing, your misfortune has purpose. It may not appear so, but if you can hold on a little while longer, God will do something powerful in your life. He will make you greater and bless you and your household substantially. The following stories drive home this point.

The Throes of Financial Woes

What is a man to do when his financial stability crashes unexpectedly to the ground, leaving him in financial ruins? Debt. Student loans. Child. This list goes on and on.

A few days ago, I hung out with a few coworkers at lunch, discussing the latest episode of our favorite evening drama. Later on I received a call from the corporate office, letting me know that my services were no longer needed. No longer needed? Really? Why me?

I drove home infuriated, replaying the call in my mind. "Your services are no longer needed ..." Over and over again, I burdened myself with these words. I then awoke to a new reality. I no longer had an income. What about my child? He required clothes, food and shelter. What about the mortgage and car note? We needed a place to live and a way to get him to his doctor appointments.

The dunghill of bad thoughts grew exponentially. Somehow I had to overcome this. Somehow I needed a way out. New job, perhaps? Start a business? But, how and with what money? I only hoped this was a bad dream from which I would awake. It wasn't. I called on God and He showed me favor—not by "fixing" the issue, but by helping me understand where I put my faith. I placed faith in a job when I should've put my faith in Him. Through this revelation, I learned to trust Him more, built a company and ensured the wellbeing of my family.

The above story emphasizes the importance of relying on God in the absence of financial security. Like many obstacles, financial adversity is conquerable. Just remember that God will make a way for you during unfavorable conditions.

Perhaps financial instability is not your misfortune. Maybe your misfortune is the death of a loved one. You may ask, "Can God heal my heart when I blame Him for my loss?" The following story may help answer your question.

It Shook My Faith

August 20, 2014. It's a day I'll never forget—one which will forever haunt me.

On the weekend of August 3, 2014, my sister called me to discuss the cost and particulars of our mother's 53rd birthday celebration. Living nearly 3,000 miles away, I happily played my part financially to ensure she would have a great time.

She did. My sister sent me videos and pictures of my mother getting pampered, dancing and having a good time. I wished I could've been there. I should have been.

I called my mother on the morning of her birthday, August 3rd. She thanked me and said, "Baby, it was the best birthday I ever had. I love you all so much!"

"I'm glad you had a good time," I smiled. "I love you too!"

My mother and I ended our conversation after speaking about her wonderful weekend.

In the afternoon of August 4th, I called my mother for our routine chit-chat about life. I needed her advice on a situation I was undergoing. Sounding out-of-breath, she said she'll call me back after her breathing treatment. "Okay woman," I said. "Call me later."

I thought nothing of my mother's shortness of breath. It was normal following an active weekend. Presuming she was tired, as normal, I gave no thought about her not calling me back. I'd call her tomorrow, I thought.

Then came August 5th. I received a call from my sister. Her voice was absent of the joy and excitement I heard a few days prior.

"Ellard! Ellard!" my sister hollered.

"Calm down sis, what is it?" I asked.

"Mom had an acute asthma attack, which led to cardiac arrest," she whined. "She's in critical condition at the hospital ..."

I nearly dropped the phone. I had just talked to my mother several hours ago.

Unaware of the severity of the situation, I had my sister send me pictures. The ghastly sight nearly sent me into shock. Immediately, I requested my wife to find us plane tickets.

Upon touching down in the evening of August 6th, I rushed to the hospital, hoping my mother would greet me. She didn't, only a few family members.

Standing next to her hospital bed, I prayed to God for her healing. I prayed it was a dream. It wasn't. My mother lay non-responsive with tubes running from her mouth to a machine. I couldn't believe my eyes. The doctors informed me that she suffered from brain damage and may never recover. I refused to believe their words.

Each day I spoke to my mother, prayed with her, and believed she would awake. My siblings, wife and extended family watched as I ministered to, and cried over, her. She opened her eyes slightly, slowly moving her head from the left to the right. Progress I thought.

Then came the evening of August 20th. I left the hospital early evening to give my son a bath at my sister's house. While bathing him, my phone rang.

"Ellard," my sister cried hysterically. "Mom's gone!"

"What ..."

I couldn't understand. I had only been gone for a couple hours. Emotionally rattled, I couldn't breathe. I couldn't talk. I cried uncontrollably. A few hours prior to this unfortunate news I told my mother that I would see her tomorrow. I never knew tomorrow wouldn't come ...

Faith shaken, I tried to collect my thoughts and prepare for my mother's funeral, scheduled a week later. Since she didn't have a church home, I decided to eulogize her. But how would I do this? Friends and family questioned my ability. I believe I did too. I had no other choice. No pastor knew her better than her son. Besides, she would've wanted me to.

On August 30th, I gave my mother the proper home-going service she deserved. "Exceptional Woman!" She would've been proud. Following the sermon, friends praised and congratulated me. "Don't thank me," I thought as I stared at my mother's body one last time, feeling empty, knowing I would never again get her motherly advice and affection.

Months following the ceremony, I still find myself weeping in the mirror, asking God how to move forward. My best friend was taken away from me. Although I believe in Him, and His healing power, I tell Him to help me understand. Why God? Why? How can you take my mother without warning? What have I done for this to happen?

The frequently quoted Romans 8:28^KJV scripture filled my mind. "All things work together for the good of them who love God, to them who are called according to His purpose." Unfortunately, it raised more questions instead of answers. Was the pain and hurt His purpose? And if so, what am I "called" to do?

I soon became unmotivated, caring about nothing. Work? Who cared? Then I remembered my mother: "Baby, make sure you accomplish your dreams, and take care of El Boogie (my son) and your wife!" Upon hearing her voice, I push myself each day, asking her and God for the strength to move forward. Daily I embrace my wife and child as they are my reasons for moving on. "Mom, I promise to make you proud! I won't give up! God, it's hard, but I trust you!"

Whether your form of misfortune is illness, the death of a loved one, or financial loss, it's to prepare you for something greater. The devastation may make moving forward difficult, but you cannot quit. Do not give Satan the satisfaction of seeing you fall. Rather, endure each hardship as a good soldier and continue to "press toward the mark for the prize of the high calling of God in Christ Jesus" (Philippians 3:14[KJV]).

The Goliath of the Past

Forget the former things; do not dwell on the past.

– Isaiah 43:18[NIV]

We often spend valuable time in fruitless or unproductive activities. This includes thinking about actions we would've, should've, or could've taken in our past. We can do nothing about yesterday. Embrace it. Yes, we did make mistakes. Yes, we did have good times. Yes, we did love our exes. Yet, whatever you did, and didn't do, cannot stand in the way of your destiny.

Remembering the Good Ol' Days

> "Nothing could be better than this," I thought, standing on my balcony. "Women … money … what else could a man ask for? I had finally made it."
>
> Well, that was years ago. I am now trying to determine my next move. What is a man to do? Things for me may never be better than what they were. I never knew that a bad investment would ruin me financially. I had a nice house, impressive bank account balances and the opportunity to travel as I pleased. It's now all gone.

> Whenever my friends and constituents ask what I am doing nowadays, I reply, "Making it happen." Truthfully, I'm making nothing happen. Each day I find myself encamped in the memories of the good ol' days. I wish I could go back to how things were! I wish I could go back to that place where I was successful—to be somebody of worth! If only I could go back in time …

Have you ever dreamt about a do-over? Ever imagined going back to that place when you were "some body of worth"? How about going back to an ex-girlfriend, ex-boyfriend or ex-spouse?

Operating under the duress, or euphoria, of your past holds no value. Unless it propels you forward, it's useless. Each unproductive moment spent in past memories lessens the time you have to construct your future. Think of your past as nothing more than a teacher and each experience a lesson.

In the Book of Philippians, Apostle Paul says something astounding about how we should see the past: "Forgetting what lies behind and reaching forward to what lies ahead"(Philippians 3:13[NASB]). The scripture reminds us about the importance of moving forward rather than focusing on the past. This requires forgetting about the good times you shared with an ex-lover; forgetting about the mistakes you made; forgetting about the time you had it all; and forgetting about the opportunities you failed to take. Dwelling on past matters is an unproductive task.

While operating in this life, it's important to understand that God is a Deity of advancement. Everything He does in your life contributes to progress. This includes the opportunities in your now, and those waiting in your tomorrow. Mark 12:27[KJV] states, "He is not the God of the dead, but the God of the living ..."

Symbolically, the word "dead" in the scripture indicates your past; the word "living" identifies your future as a breathing, living entity. If God focuses on advancement, then you must make moving forward a priority in your life. Jesus exemplifies how we ought to proceed, despite transgressions.

When Jesus had to carry the cross, He did so for our salvation, our redemption and our sins. He didn't think about the good times of His youth. He didn't spend long hours in unproductive thoughts about 'what if' scenarios. He instead remained focused on redeeming us to God—His purpose. Knowing about the suffering, beatings, ridiculing, abandonment, affliction and crucifixion He would endure, Christ pressed forward. Through hardship, He pressed forward. Through ridicule, He pressed forward. Through betrayal, He pressed forward. Through agony and misery ... He pressed forward. Our Lord and Savior died to ensure we could have a future. We should thank Him by following His example and walking in the purpose God has for us. Despite what anyone may have said or done to you, lift your head and move forward.

No matter how great or damaging your past is, you can move forward. Your promise, vision and mission await you. How long depends solely on you. Here's something to remember. Your past pales in comparison to the future God have waiting for you.

The Goliath of "Self"

For I say to every man that is among you, through the grace given unto me, not to think of himself more highly than he ought to think, but to think soberly according as God hath dealt to every man the measure of faith.

– Romans 12:3KJV

A great giant, perhaps greater than any other giant, is the Goliath of "self." Yes, the person with whom you go to sleep, and to whom you awake, may be stopping you from higher achievement, success and happiness. Yes, this beautiful woman or handsome man may be the reason you're not operating in purpose or destiny.

Some may disagree with the previous statement. If you're one who disagrees, consider the common factor in everything you do. If you choose to give up on your vision, goals or dreams, who's making the choice? You. If you become distracted, who's giving away your attention? You. If you choose not to fulfill the purpose God gave you, with whom does the fault lie? You. If you let past mistakes impede your progress, with whom should agitation be directed? You.

You have the power to determine how successful, or unsuccessful, you become. Some may ask, "How is this possible when I constantly face challenges?"

We grow and develop through the introduction to numerous experiences; some good and some unfavorable. These experiences then impact what we do, how we do and why we do. As time progresses, these ways of thinking, or adopted thought patterns, become set in our subconscious mind. This adoption then dictates the next words we speak or subsequent actions we take.

When God drops purpose in your spirit, or gives you a great idea, you may become reluctant to act on it. This usually occurs because His will often conflicts with your own feelings, desires or ambitions. Consider the Prophet Jonah as an example.

> Jonah receives the call from the Lord to preach repentance to the people of Nineveh—a people dejected by God for their cruelty, inhumane conduct and wickedness (Jonah 1:1).
>
> Loyal to Israel, Jonah despised any enemy of his people, especially the Ninevites. Yet, when God directs Jonah to preach to Nineveh, he refuses and decides to head in a different direction (Jonah 1:3).
>
> Relying on his own understanding and opposing God's direction, Jonah discovers how powerful God's will for his life than his own becomes.
>
> As Jonah relaxes on a ship, heading to Tarshish (a place very far from Nineveh), God causes a storm to threaten the livelihood of each person on the vessel. The seamen pray to their gods and encourage Jonah to do the same. Following frantic dialogue, the men discover Jonah's disobedience as the cause for the storm. Desiring no further harm to the men, Jonah advises them to throw him overboard.

> Upon the men's decision, God creates a great fish to swallow up Jonah in which he resides and pleads with God for three days for forgiveness.
>
> – Book of Jonah

The 'self' is an intelligent and fallible being. It's often characterized as egocentric, ambitious, opportunistic, avaricious and arrogant. Sadly, the 'self' often misleads people to believing themselves as gods. God detests this path of thinking (Exodus 20:3; Matthew 6:24).

When God calls you to do great works, you must abandon your personal ambitions, agendas, reluctances and prejudices. Your will cannot take precedence over His purpose for your life. Relinquish self-driven motives. Calm your emotions. Remove self-defeating thoughts from your mind. Once you align your desires with God's plan, He will cause you to receive, "abundantly above all you can ask or think, according to the power that works in you" (Ephesians 3:20[KJV]). Do not let the 'self' ruin your chances at a prosperous, fulfilling and productive future.

Goliath of Addiction

No temptation has overtaken you except such as is common to man; but God is faithful, who will not allow you to be tempted beyond what you are able, but with the temptation will also make the way of escape, that you may be able to bear it.

– 1 Corinthians 10:13[KJV]

Most people believe addictions to be tied only to drugs and alcohol. Nothing could be further from the truth. An addiction by definition is "the state of being enslaved to a habit or practice or to something that is psychologically or physically habit-forming ..." Additionally, it's anything or anyone that occupies your time extensively, dominates your mind constantly or manipulates your emotions to the extent you lose the ability to say "no." Once consumed, or intoxicated, you may divert from God and His purpose for your life.

The power of addiction is expressed eloquently through King David's oldest son, Amnon. The story reveals how uncontrollable desires can lead to an unfortunate demise.

> Amnon had an unnatural, strong sexual longing for his virgin sister, Tamar. The strength and intensity of his avidity had become unbreakable. Pondering ways to manifest his impure thoughts, he discusses the matter over with his friend and cousin Jonadab. Realizing Amnon's overwhelming passion to have Tamar, Jonadab gives him a "good" idea: lie down in bed, act sick and request Tamar to come take care of him. Overcome by lust, Amnon follows Jonadab's advice.
>
> When Tamar arrives to Amnon's room, the unthinkable occurs. Amnon presents himself healthy, and attempts to seduce her—to fulfill his sexual caprices. Tamar, however, denies Amnon's advances and urges him to change his mind. Driven by his own desires, he ignores his sister's plea and rapes her, showing no remorse for his uncompassionate actions.

Upon climax, or getting his "fix," Amnon rudely dismisses Tamar from his sight, leaving her emotionally scarred and abandoned. Conquest complete, Amnon could never imagine the consequences awaiting him in the future. Two years later, he is killed for his heinous act by Tamara's other brother, Absolom (2 Samuel 13: 1- 18; 2 Samuel 13: 23 - 28).

We're often oblivious to the consequences of our actions when consumed by our own "needs," or blinded by our own desires. We unfortunately jeopardize purpose and destiny for something, or for someone, with no value to add to our life. The following story exposes how one man's addiction nearly cost his livelihood.

The Casino Man

Gambling had been Kevin's outlet since he learned how in the alley with his friends. Sometimes he could control it; other times it got the best of him. This particular night, he got more than he had expected.

Driven by emotions, Kevin heads to the casino. Upon entering the facility he inhales deeply, taking in the sounds of slot machines, clapping and people chatting. "This will be a good night," Kevin says, walking towards the Black Jack table.

Within minutes, Kevin loses several hands. "This is ridiculous," he says. Opening his wallet, he retrieves

> another $100, believing he can recover from previous losses …
>
> Kevin spends hours at the table, trying to win back his initial $100. This chase leads him down a dark, financial pit from which he cannot climb. Following several trips to the ATM, Kevin decides to leave, feeling sick to his stomach, thousands given over to the casino. "How could I be so foolish," Kevin sighs, thinking about the debt he had created in one evening.
>
> Although Kevin suffers a large financial loss, he returns the next day to the casino with high hopes of breaking even. He doesn't—only more debt.

Many of us have an addiction of some sort. Whomever or whatever we're controlled by becomes our god. Whether your addiction is to drugs and alcohol; to working excessively; to promiscuity; to pleasing people; to lying; to cheating; to stealing; to fame; to gossip; to constant worry; to complaining, or to "getting" money, your struggle is obstructing the future God has for you. Unfortunately, many of us do not realize we're under the spell of addiction until an area in our life becomes negatively impacted.

Some people lose relationships, incur health challenges and face self-afflicted losses before they realize the presence of an addiction. Others may discover it through expressed concern by friends, family, or therapists. One way to identify if addictions exist is to complete the "Am I Addicted" questionnaire.

Am I Addicted

- Have you ever felt a need to minimize or cut down on your indulgences? [Y/N]
- Have you ever become annoyed when criticized about your activities or behaviors? [Y/N]
- Have you ever been overcome by guilt for engaging in certain activities too long? [Y/N]
- Are you willing to do anything, by any means necessary, to fulfill your urges? [Y/N]
- Have you hurt others in the wake of your escapades to ensure your own "needs"? [Y/N]
- Is this activity or person requiring the majority of your time, energy and resources? [Y/N]
- Does this force keep you from fulfilling God's plan for your life? [Y/N]

Answering "yes" to one or more of these questions may mean you have an addiction to something or someone. Do not be ashamed. You are not alone!

Addictions have become giants for countless people. They have stopped them from achieving purpose and operating in destiny. Since you are a person of greatness, God doesn't want anything to rule over you. He desires you free from the control and bondage of your struggle. Thus, if you're going to break the hold of your addiction, you must let Him know about your weaknesses. Be honest and open. Tell Him you're attached to someone or something. He in turn will set you on a path of deliverance and breakthrough.

Giants Do Not Come To Destroy You

Yet destroyed I the Amorite before them, whose height *was* like the height of the cedars, and he *was* strong as the oaks; yet I destroyed his fruit from above, and his roots from beneath.

–Amos 2:9[KJV]

The giants, or Goliaths, in your life are not created to destroy you. As you consider the hell, challenges, turmoil and anguish you had experienced, or undergoing currently, you may disagree with this statement. Your feelings are duly noted.

Rather than break you down, the nuances and obstacles come to prepare you for your next level. Most people would never take action unless pushed. God knows this. As your next level in life requires greater courage, greater faith, and greater trust in Him, God has to provoke you to leave the state of complacency and comfort. Before you think yourself incapable of overcoming your Goliaths, remember this scripture: "I can do all things through Christ who strengthens me" (Philippians 4:13[NKJV]). Your strength then doesn't come from you, but from Jesus.

Despite where you are in life, you have within you a giant killer—a courageous warrior. This person needs only to be activated. Now is the time to summon this powerful and incredible person.

Two

Activate Your David

And as he [David] talked with them [men of Israel], behold, there came up the champion, the Philistine of Gath, Goliath by name, out of the armies of the Philistines, and spake [spoke] according to the same words: and David heard them.

–1 Samuel 17:23[KJV], emphasis added

Opposition is God's activation code to your greater self. In other words, it's to provoke your inner David. This individual emerges in the wake of hardships and says, "I will overcome!" This person rises as a phoenix amid possible defeat and says, "I will become triumphant!" Your time to bring out your warrior has come.

Israel's failure to challenge Goliath pushed God to choose His own warrior. Unlike King Saul, this person would possess unflinching courage, exude admirable obedience and demonstrate strategic ability. His choice: David.

Who was David?

To his father, David was the youngest son and the caretaker of the family's sheep. To his brothers, he was merely the little brother who had little significance. To God, however, David was a divine response to opposition in the absence of courageous men.

The altercation between Goliath and the men of Israel presented an opportunity for the king and his men to showcase their own combat skill. Oddly, no one accepted the challenge. Although the men of Israel feared Goliath, King Saul could've contended with the giant, but he didn't. Why is this?

Saul's cowardly display may stem from 1 Samuel 15. Due to his disobedience, God removed His Spirit from him. Without the Spirit of God, Saul would have to rely on his own ability to achieve Godly results. Defeating Goliath was a task only achievable with God. **Achieving Godly results without God is impossible**.

Acquiring Godly results without the Spirit of God does not exist. Only through God's direction and His power can any quantifiable measurement of success occur. Only through God can we become victorious over the enemy and his attacks. Only through Him can we surmount difficult and emotionally crushing moments. Only through His help will giants meet their demise.

When Saul lost God's favor, God shifted His focus to someone else with more desirable qualities: David. God's choice would appear odd because many would discount the young man for a few reasons.

1. David didn't come from a royal family. How then would he earn people's respect?

2. David wasn't skilled in the art of organized warfare. His lack of military knowledge would disqualify him from being a "brother in arms" amongst the king's men.
3. David's youthfulness suggested him to be inexperienced. Who then would follow a child?

With odds stacked heavily against young David, what about him captivated God? Why wouldn't God choose someone else that appeared "kinglier" or "worthier" to rectify the pressing matter?

Characteristics of David

And when he had removed him, He raised up unto them David to be their king; to whom also he gave their testimony, and said, I have found David the son of Jesse, a man after mine own heart, which shall fulfill all my will.

– Acts 13:22[KJV]

Character examination of David reveals several qualities and attributes that attracted God's attention. Whereas most people would have considered him an unworthy pick, God saw something greater in the young man.

I. He loved God

Let the words of my mouth, and the meditation of my heart, be acceptable in thy sight, O LORD, my strength, and my redeemer.

– Psalms 19:14[KJV]

David's faith, strength and courage stemmed from his tight-knit relationship with God. At a young age, David pursued to understand God's heart, His desires and His ways. The moments spent in the wilderness, while protecting his father's sheep, for example, was David's worship and fellowship time. Although there's no mention of this relationship during Israel's altercation with Goliath, David expresses his undying love for God through one of his many Psalms: Psalm 63[NIV].

> 1 You, God, are my God,
> earnestly I seek you;
> I thirst for you,
> my whole being longs for you,
> in a dry and parched land
> where there is no water.
>
> 2 I have seen you in the sanctuary
> and beheld your power and your glory.
> 3 Because your love is better than life,
> my lips will glorify you.
> 4 I will praise you as long as I live,
> and in your name I will lift up my hands.
> 5 I will be fully satisfied as with the richest of foods;
> with singing lips my mouth will praise you.
>
> 6 On my bed I remember you;
> I think of you through the watches of the night.
> 7 Because you are my help,
> I sing in the shadow of your wings.

8 I cling to you;
your right hand upholds me.

9 Those who want to kill me will be destroyed;
they will go down to the depths of the earth.
10 They will be given over to the sword
and become food for jackals.

11 But the king will rejoice in God;
all who swear by God will glory in him,
while the mouths of liars will be silenced.

Having a relationship with God is critical to your future. It establishes your destiny and opens up the doors to promise and vision. God reveals His innermost desires and His mission for your life through relationship. As with any father, God craves intimacy with you. Despite the madness you endure, He wants you to know that He's there for you. Sometimes you may feel abandoned during your challenges, but don't fret. He's an ever-present help in times of trouble (Psalms 46:1).

How strong is your relationship with God? Do you study His Word? Do you worship Him? Do you "enter into His gates with thanksgiving, and into His courts with praise" as stated in Psalms 100:4[KJV]. If you feel you've fallen short in this area, take time to repent and ask God to reestablish you. Your anointing and greatness append on a strong relationship with the Heavenly Father.

II. He was accountable

And whatsoever ye do, do it heartily, as to the Lord, and not unto men.

– Colossians 3:23KJV

God wants an abundant life for you. He also desires you to be prepared to give an account for the opportunities you took or did not take. God holds you accountable for every idea and vision He gives you.

David possessed a high level of accountability. His uncompromising commitment to responsibility was admirable. As the youngest son, he inherited the role of shepherd over his father's sheep. This position required humility and came with many risks. Without complaining, David served in this capacity despite the dangers that awaited him (1 Samuel 16:11). What dangers could've faced David?

Bobcats, coyotes, wolves, lions, and bears are common predators of sheep. As the shepherd, David had to be prepared for a number of attacks. Committed to his responsibility, he risked his life daily to protect the lives of his father's investment.

Why does God love people with accountability? Why does He pour favor upon those who possess it? There are several reasons.

Firstly, accountability exposes a person's level of commitment. God perceives an individual without accountability as undisciplined and uncommitted. God seldom entrusts purpose or vision to individuals lacking this attribute. James 1:8KJV substantiates, "A double-minded mind is unstable in all his ways." Where there's no accountability there's no commitment.

Secondly, accountability is the trademark of excellence. Every person established in greatness by God either possessed, or developed, this magnetic quality. Accountability then suggests individual ownership of mistakes rather than passing the buck or finger pointing. Greatness cannot be achieved by being passive; only by embracing the outcome of your decisions. Ezra 10:4[NASB] inspires, "Arise, for this matter is your responsibility ... Be of good courage, and do it." If you desire God's favor in your life, increase your level of accountability.

Thirdly, accountability determines or exposes a person's trustworthiness and creditability. Since God desires you to walk in the strength of your purpose, you must be reliable. Reliability is built by following through, or making good, on whatever you speak. Ecclesiastes 7:1[NIV] notes, "A good name is better than fine perfume ..." Everything you do, or fail to do, is connected to your name. When people speak your name, do they associate you with being trustworthy and creditable, or as unreliable?

Accountability is essential to your destiny. Although God wants to ignite your life with purpose, you first must strengthen your level of accountability. How accountable have you been to the people, opportunities, ideas and the vision God has placed before you? Be honest. Is there room for improvement? Great opportunities will welcome you once your accountability score with God rises.

III. He represented a new beginning

A new heart also will I give you, and a new spirit will I put within you: and I will take away the stony heart out of your flesh, and I will give you a heart of flesh.

– Ezekiel 36:26KJV

As Jesse's eighth and youngest son, David represented a new beginning in the lineage of his father and Israel. Through him, people would find hope amidst the ruins of adverse circumstances. Through him, our Lord and Savior Jesus Christ would become a descendant (John 7:42). Through him, powerful songs about God would become written. Through him, God would create a new kingdom and powerful legacy.

In the spiritual realm, the number eight, "sh'moneh" in Hebrew, from the root "shah'meyn" means the number of salvation, resurrection and new birth (or new beginnings). Usually when God initiates a new beginning, He chooses someone receptive to His direction, unmoved by people's negative thoughts or opinions, and who possesses obedience, selflessness, and fearlessness. David encompassed all these traits. You do too!

God desires a new beginning in your life. Despite what people may think or say, you're greater than what your socioeconomic status suggests. You're more powerful than what your past indicates. David's father may have seen him only fit to watch sheep (and to his brothers an insignificant person), but God saw a king. Job 8:7NIV encourages, "Your beginnings will seem humble, so prosperous will your future be."

Your life is about to change for the better. The undercurrent of anguish you experienced was necessary for something new to occur. Out of all the people God could've chosen, He set His affections on you. He cares nothing about your past mistakes or how others may see you. He wants you to excel in the life He has given you. As He continues to shape you, people will see your unimaginable transformation from who you were to who you're destined to become.

IV. He opposed the status quo

For when the priesthood is changed, the law must be changed also.

– Hebrews 7:12[NIV]

A divine change, or shift, must occur during disobedience and apathy. God finds these behaviors offensive and will set in order an atmosphere or an environment in disarray. Saul's past disobedience (and his recent failure to face Goliath) led to his inevitable replacement.

In 1 Samuel 16, God informs the prophet Samuel of His intentions for a new king. "Fill your horn with oil and be on your way; I am sending you to Jesse of Bethlehem. I have chosen one of his sons to be king" (1 Samuel 16:1[NIV]).

> Upon arriving at Jesse's house, Samuel interviews Jesse's eldest son, Eliab—a young, tall and handsome man. Mesmerized by the handsome young man, Samuel says, "Surely, the Lord's anointed is before him." Before he could proceed, God immediately responds, "Look not

> on his countenance [appearance] or on the height of his stature; because I have refused [rejected] him: for the LORD seeth not as man seeth [see]; for man looketh on the outward appearance, but the LORD looketh on the heart" (1 Samuel 16:7[KJV], emphasis added).
>
> Following God's words, Samuel interviews the other six sons. Despite the men's attractiveness and their level of intellectual prowess, neither son is chosen.
>
> After reviewing the seven men, Samuel asks Jesse a very interesting question: "Are all the young men here?" Reluctantly, Jesse responds, "There remains yet the youngest, and there he is, keeping the sheep" (1 Samuel 16:8[NKJV]). Samuel replies, "Send and bring him. For we will not sit down till he comes here."
>
> Jesse brings David into the house, presents him to Samuel. Strangely, he did not familiar his brothers. Although handsome as they were, he was ruddy (red) and rough. And as he stands before Samuel, God tells the prophet to "Rise and anoint him; this is the one" (1 Samuel 16:8 -12).

Whereas the other seven sons had kingly qualities, or looked the part of a king, God chose the politically untainted and rough-around-the-edges teenager. He chose someone who most people would not consider leader-worthy and least likely to become successful. He chose the one whose family felt unqualified to achieve greatness.

Despite what people think, you are God's elect. People may disqualify you for opportunities, but God says, "This is the one!" Some may say you have a checkered past, but God says, "This is the one!" You cannot get caught up in what people say or think about you. God is about to take you somewhere above each person who has ever looked down at you, talked about you, or disapproved of you. Give them no more attention. Your next level does not have room for unbelieving, negative individuals.

As you read the above scriptures, you will find something very profound about David. Unlike his brothers, David was discovered outside <u>working</u>, tending to the sheep. While his brothers were presented as his father's finest collection, David attended to his responsibilities. What does this say? God has a fondness for working people. Working people have a mission and often have a desire for something greater.

Although you may be working, you may not like where you work. Keep working. Your business may not be prospering as you'd hope, but keep working. You may feel overwhelmed with visionless, disrespectful, and unappreciative people, but keep working. You may be working a job for which you're overqualified, but keep working. Wherever you work, it's to help define and strengthen your ability, creativity and vision. Before you leave prematurely, remember this: Your humility and tenacity have gotten God's attention. That said, expect your Samuel, or opportunity, to find you. Change may happen quicker than you think.

If you have been dismissed, overlooked or rejected as David was, do not worry. God got you. He has a plan for your life! The inconsiderate family members, negative friends or disbelieving constituents were necessary to put you where God needs you. Regardless where you are in life, you are in the right place. God is about to set you afoot to greatness. The value others cannot see in you shines brightly to Him. Although David was not his "father's choice," he was "The Father's" choice! You are no different.

V. He was obedient

But he said, "Yea rather, blessed are they that hear the word of God, and keep it.

– Luke 11:28KJV

Adding to David's roster of impressive attributes, he possessed the spirit of obedience. As a good child, he did everything his father requested, without complaining or whining. Looking after the sheep, for example, was not the most enticing job, but David did it. Another fatherly request, nonetheless, would place him in the environment where God predestined him to be. This is revealed in 1 Samuel 17:17-19.

> While speaking to David, Jesse says, "Take this ephah [bushel] of roasted grain and these ten loaves of bread for your brothers and hurry to their camp. Take along these ten cheeses to the commander of their unit. See how your brothers are and bring back some assurance from them. They are with Saul and all the men of Israel in the Valley of Elah, fighting against the Philistines" (1 Samuel 17:17-19NIV, emphasis added).

> Early in the morning David left the flock in the care of a shepherd, loaded up and set out, as Jesse had directed. He reached the camp as the army was going out to its battle positions, shouting the war cry. [21] Israel and the Philistines were drawing up their lines facing each other. David left his things with the keeper of supplies, ran to the battle lines and asked his brothers how they were (1 Samuel 17:20-23[NIV]).

Jesse's request may seem simple, but it reveals something intriguing about God's strategy. Notice God never tells David directly where to go, nor informs him of Israel's issue with Goliath. Instead, He uses David's father to send him to the environment where his destiny would begin. He knew the strength of David's obedience. If David had refused or disobeyed his father, he would have missed out on several opportunities.

1. He would not have been able to bring order to a hostile environment.
2. He would not have been able break Israel's perception of impossibility.
3. He would not have been able to gain economic affluence or showcase the power of God within him.

Obedience unlocks God's power and favor in your life. 1 Samuel 15:22[KJV] says, "To obey is better than sacrifice ..." Obedience then opens up the doors to opportunity. It also places you in an environment where you may discover your own destiny. Unfortunately, people who operate in disobedience often disqualify themselves from personal and professional advancement. As you look at yourself, answer this question truthfully: Are you obedient or are you a dissenter?

If you desire better and greater in your life, you must operate in the spirit and mind of obedience. This means being obedient to God's Word, obedient to your calling, obedient to the details of your purpose and obedient to the wise people God place in your life. Do not let disobedience cost your future. It's a destitution from which recovery is very difficult.

VI. He was fearless

The LORD is my light and my salvation; whom shall I fear? The LORD is the strength of my life; of whom shall I be afraid?

– Psalms 27:1[KJV]

God's vision for your life requires fearlessness. If you're to seize opportunity, you first must abandon fear. Notice the courage David possessed.

> Upon arriving to the battle site, David hears Goliath's mockery. Looking around he notices the fear in the men. Baffled, David elects himself to fight Goliath. After hearing David, the men bring him before King Saul (1 Samuel 17:16[KJV]).
>
> Standing before the king, David says with confidence, "Let no man's heart fail because of him [Goliath]; thy

> [your] servant will go and fight with this Philistine" (1 Samuel 17:32[KJV], emphasis added).

How could a young boy with no military training have more confidence than Israel's soldiers? Why didn't Goliath intimidate him as the others? Several reasons exist.

1. David's resume consisted of killing beasts larger than he. While watching over his father's sheep, he killed a bear and a lion. These animals would have mauled to death most men, but David remained victorious (1 Samuel 17:34).
2. David had unbreakable faith and relied heavily on God. The source of his power came from God, not anyone else. Thus, the presence of God ensured favorable outcomes over his attackers.
3. Fear and intimidation are learned behaviors. As the youngest of seven brothers, and as the family's shepherd, David could not exhibit such emotion. David's heroic act reminds us that fear has little value in the presence of strong opposition.

As in the case of David, God wants you to confront your challenges fearlessly. He wants you to muster up the courage to say, "Let no man's heart fail … your servant will go and fight this Philistine." Despite the giants threatening your livelihood, God has given you the strength to face them.

VII. He was gifted

A man's gift maketh room for him, and bringeth him before great men.

–Proverbs 18:16[KJV]

Spiritually-gifted people can positively influence their surroundings and those with whom they come in contact. Proverbs 18:16[KJV] states, "A man's gift maketh room for him, and bringeth him before great men." Great men (and women) include people of influence, those holding key positions, and, in David's case, the king.

> Once God removed His Spirit from Saul, He sent an evil spirit, or the spirit of misery, to afflict him (1 Samuel 16:14). Noticing Saul's defunctive or sad nature, a group of his servants discuss ways they could assist the king. Following a conference, they conclude David (and his skillful play of the harp), as the king's remedy. In agreement, the men summon the young man.
>
> David's musicianship complimented his fighting ability. His playing of the harp caused shifts in the environments. Moods changed. Spiritual attacks ceased. Each time God afflicted the king, David played beautifully until Saul had become emotionally restored (1 Samuel 16:14-18; 1 Samuel 16:23).

You are a gifted individual. God has given you the ability to shift climates and impact positively the people you encounter. Your gift will sharpen minds, restore hope and cause dreams to manifest. Through your gift, you will become the change agent in the lives of "great men (and women)."

It is time for you to cause a shift in your life and in the life of others. Whether your gift is musicianship, speaking, acting, singing, poetry, writing, praying, preaching, evangelism, or entrepreneurship, it is to help those afflicted, or in need of your skills. Do not let another day pass by without using your gift. People need you.

The David in You

And David became more and more powerful, because the LORD Almighty was with him.

–1 Chronicles 11:9NIV

Up to this point in your life, you had to face numerous challenges. Some should've killed you, literally. Others may have crushed you emotionally, spiritually or financially. Despite their damages, however, you're still here. God sees it fit to keep you. Have you ever asked why?

You're here to be a testimony. The giant you kill will empower your friends, family and many others to do something extraordinary—to achieve greater in their own lives. The David within you is the answer to their situation. Take for example this courageous young woman.

I am not DISABLED

> People thought that her illness would prevent her from having a child or getting married—from opening a business—from academic advancement. According to unbelievers, she would never have a happy life. But she does!
>
> Dawn has baffled naysayers for years. Whenever someone said she couldn't do something, she did it with a queenly flair. Despite her illness, Dawn runs her own business, mothers a child, has a loving husband, has several degrees, and is an inspiration to her community. Whereas many people with the same condition had given up, Dawn grabs life by the horns—maximizing every second. How does she do it? She doesn't let her illness put limitations on her life.

Your Davidic spirit does not know defeat. It opposes self-victimizing thoughts. It does not recognize inadequacy and rejects feelings of insignificance.

The enemy wants you to see your challenges as disadvantages, but they're not. Pastor Dr. Kevin Williams, a phenomenal and highly respected leader in the community, once said, "You don't have disadvantages; you just have different advantages."

You're not at a disadvantage because you have adversity in your life. Rather you're at an advantage because you had to learn how to maneuver in a merciless world that has tagged you as unfortunate or disabled. "But what the enemy meant for evil, God meant for your good" (Genesis 50:20[KJV]).

The next story reveals how one family overcame the odds of bringing a new life into the world, baffling many medical professionals.

A Prevailing Mother

The birth of my child had been anything but an easy journey. According to some doctors, he wasn't supposed to live; but God showed my wife and me favor.

According to many, my wife's battle with sickle cell disease would prevent her from experiencing the joys of motherhood. She may have accepted this nonsense for a brief moment, but in mid-2012, we got pregnant.

Carrying a child was rough on my wife's body. Excruciating pains and several hospitalizations attempted to claim both her life and the life she carried. Refusing to give up, she fought back with a vengeance, perceiving victory over the situation. "I will carry this child full-term," she said. "I will prevail!"

Relying on God, and after thirty eight weeks of challenges—to include emotional anguish, blood transfusions and restless nights—my wife and I gave birth to a healthy baby boy: Ellard Thomas, II. My wife not only survived the birth, she conquered it. By God's grace and through her resilient spirit, I am a proud father. Thank you Jesus! Thank you Jesus!

The blessings waiting for you are immeasurable and tailored only for you. Many people may never understand the calling God has on your life or the situations you must endure. It doesn't matter. God's plan doesn't require their understanding. And as you operate in your inner David, you'll come to learn that opposition becomes opportunity. Adverse situations become attractions. Unfortunate circumstances become breakthroughs.

Despite how intimidating your situations may appear, you can and will stand triumphantly. Dwelling within you is a gifted, fearless, and anointed individual with the strength to do amazing deeds. As a purpose-driven, destiny-focused and vision-centric person, you will stifle doubters and baffle naysayers. As long as God guides you, you will make fear-filled people reconsider their definition of impossibility. Remember this key point: There are no unwinnable odds when you activate your David.

Three

Strategize Your Victory

So it was, when the Philistine arose and came and drew near to meet David, that David hurried and ran toward the army to meet the Philistine. [49] Then David put his hand in his bag and took out a stone; and he slung *it* and struck the Philistine in his forehead, so that the stone sank into his forehead, and he fell on his face to the earth. [50] So David prevailed over the Philistine with a sling and a stone, and struck the Philistine and killed him. But *there was* no sword in the hand of David. [51] Therefore David ran and stood over the Philistine, took his sword and drew it out of its sheath and killed him, and cut off his head with it.

–1 Samuel 17: 48-51[NKJV]

An effective strategy is important to achieving victory over your Goliath. Fulfilling your purpose requires a strategy. Manifesting your vision requires a strategy. Your success, happiness and desires require strategy. Everything you ever hope to attain requires—yes—a strategy. The lack of having one will inevitably result in defeat, disappointment or dissonance.

Some may ask, and rightfully so, "Why is having a strategy important?"

Strategy is important for three reasons:

1. **Showcases understanding:** Strategy helps you develop a clearer understanding of where you are and what's required for your ultimate success. This includes an assessment of your capabilities, identification of your strengths, realization of opposition, and knowledge of the areas you'll need assistance.
2. **Exposes adaptive opportunity**: Visual analysis of your internal and external environment reveals the speed at which you can adapt to challenges. Most people experience defeat or failure because they cannot adapt quickly to the shifts in their lives.
3. **Increases visibility and direction:** An effective strategy helps you to actualize your victory, or end result. It keeps you engaged and in-tune with your purpose and destination. Without a specific focus, or defined target to achieve, success at any level is highly improbable.

God created every great wonder through strategy. The world, you, your gift and your destiny are results of His strategic plan. If God believes in the power of strategy, we, too, must have one for our own lives.

Identifying and Implementing the Strategy of David

For waging war you need guidance, and for victory many advisers.
–Proverbs 24:6[NIV]

During the confrontation with Goliath, David never approached the giant foolishly. He had a plan. But here's a question for the forward thinker. If two opposing forces both operate in the power of strategy, as in the case with David and Goliath, which one will dominate?

The battle between David and Goliath exposes two strategies at work: Goliath's and David's—one inferior and the other superior.

Goliath's strategy involved terrorizing through intimidation, belittling through insults and relying on his brute strength and undefeated record. These are the same antiquated, or old, techniques by which your current situations and circumstances want to defeat you. Although effective on the Israelites, and perhaps on many previous foes, Goliath's strategy proved ineffective and inferior to David's.

David's strategy, on the other hand, required a more systematic approach. Since Goliath wasn't a normal man, or any ordinary warrior, David had to be strategic. Based on Goliath's size, armor and weaponry, David couldn't engage him as a common soldier. Instead, he followed eight powerful and actionable steps to acquire victory. These are the same time-tested and proven methods you may use to defeat your own giants.

The Strategy of David

I. Build and Maintain a Relationship with God

You shall love the LORD your God with all your heart, with all your soul, and with all your mind.

–Matthew 22:37[NKJV]

The genesis, or beginning, of an effective strategy requires a relationship with God. As the orchestrator of your life, God has pertinent knowledge to ensure the fruition of your purpose. A strategy absent of God seals your demise. David understood this well.

If you desire to defeat your giant, make a relationship with God a top priority. David's impressive strength, unbreakable confidence and fighting ability stemmed from his close relationship with the Lord. There are many accounts that portray his undying love for God.

In 1 Samuel 13, for example, the prophet Samuel and King Saul had a conversation about the king's disobedience. During this dialogue, Samuel informs Saul about the inevitable end of his kingdom and says, "The LORD has sought out a man after his own heart and appointed him ruler of his people, because you have not kept the LORD's command" (1 Samuel 13:14[KJV]). This account is paralleled in Luke's record in Acts 13:22[ESV]: "And when He had removed him [Saul], He raised up for them [Israel] David as king, to whom also He gave testimony and said, 'I have found David the son of Jesse, a man after My own heart, who will do all My will.'" (Emphasis added)

Being a man after God's heart isn't possible without an established relationship. Through relationship, God destined David to be king. Through relationship, God gives blueprints and strategies for long-term success. Consider this. Before Goliath had become an issue, God had already intended David to be a prosperous, fearless and legendary leader.

How is your relationship with God?

Some people fret over this question. Either they're unsure or unaware of their relationship with Him. Why is this?

Relationship requires more than going to church, reading the Bible periodically, performing good deeds inconsistently and claiming to know Him. Both conviction and consistency are required.

David had a sincere drive to know God. He had a strong conviction of God's existence and worshipped Him consistently. He wanted to be in His presence. He yearned for His direction. If you'd like to grow your relationship with God, follow these steps:

> **Put God first:** Matthew 6:30 states, "Seek ye [you] first the kingdom of God and His righteousness, and all these things shall be added unto you." What things is the scripture referencing? Your innermost desires, purpose and the vision you want from God. (Emphasis added)
>
> God has no problem with giving these to you, but He wants to know if your love and affection are for Him or the gifts He can provide. Too often we fall in love with

the gifts and fail to acknowledge and respect the Giver. If God isn't sought after first and foremost, do not expect His response to your requests.

Develop a strong desire for His Word: God's Word is the action plan for your life. Each of the sixty-six books includes principles, examples, and directions to help you walk in the integrity and power of your purpose.

During your darkest moments, God's Word is the "lamp unto your feet and a light unto your path" (Psalms 119:105). During your cravings for understanding, "it's the sincere milk to help you grow" (1 Peter 2:2). When you become weakened by challenges or afflictions, it's the "power to the faint and increases your strength" (Isaiah 40:28-31).

Having a strong desire for God's Word means you understand the power it has. Through His Word, deliverance occurs. Through His Word, the grips of self-condemnation are relinquished. Through His Word, the transcendence from good to great happens. Through His Word, methods to getting healed are revealed. Through His Word, your purpose in life is given. Through His Word, God's promises and the covenant with the "believer" are released.

Individuals who have a strong desire for God's Word are driven by purpose, led by obedience and provoked by vision. When you desire God's Word, you attract His favor, His direction and His purpose for your life.

Communicate with Him often: Communication with God occurs through several methods: *efficacy of prayer, connection through confession*, and *intimacy through praise.*

Efficacy of prayer: Prayer is a powerful tool that you can use to connect with God continuously. It's the gateway of speaking to Him and getting Him to hear you. According to Jeremiah 29:12, He listens and responds to those who pray. It's through prayer that God will answer you and tell you great, unsearchable things beyond your knowledge (Jeremiah 33:3). According to Philippians 4:6, our requests are made to God through prayer.

Prayer is essential. Without prayer, you become vulnerable to the attacks of the enemy, because the line of communication from Him is cut. A severed line of communication from God creates a void, or deepens the emptiness, in your life.

Prayer proves to be a crucial activity. Jesus, for example, prayed frequently. (Matthew 14:23 & 26:36; Mark 6:46; Luke 5:16; John 17). The Apostle Paul did as well. (Romans 1:9; Ephesians 1:16). The majority of people called to do great works, or had to face strong opposition, prayed often. Thus, if you want the blessings, the favor and the guidance of God, you must "pray without ceasing."

Connection through confession: None of us like to admit our struggles, our faults or our failures. We would rather use excuses or deny them completely. No one needs to know our "secrets." Although we may not expose the dark areas of our life to anyone, we must reveal them to God.

Some may ask, "Why must I confess to God when He already knows about my internal challenges?"

Confession mobilizes God's response to your struggles. It says, "I know the error of my ways and I need you to help me!"

Many people believe confession to be unnecessary because God already knows about their circumstances. Yes, God does know. However, deliverance cannot occur as long as there is a desire to defend your sin, or continue to perform ungodly behaviors.

If you have a struggle, or find yourself doing activities that you want to quit, confess them to God. He will respond. "If we confess our sins, He is faithful and just to forgive us *our* sins, and to cleanse us from all unrighteousness" (1 John 1:9[KJV]).

***Intimacy through praise*:** Praise is another important element to bring you closer to God. It elevates you into His presence, His love and His power. It signifies your level of devotion to Him.

God enjoys praise, as it is an expression of worship. When He is exalted or lifted up, regardless of your circumstances, it draws Him closer to you. Praise says:

"Lord no matter what I'm undergoing, I thank you!"

"God I love you and I trust you!"

"God I thank you for all you've done, what you're doing and what you're going to do!"

"God although I don't understand what I'm experiencing, I know you are able!"

It's unfortunate that many people do not know what praise is. Therefore, they never experience the feeling of being in God's presence. That said, let's define this God-attracting activity.

Praise is "to commend, to applaud or magnify." It is a joyful recounting of all that God has done, what He's doing and all He's going to do. It's a sincere and truthful acknowledgement of His divine acts through singing, dancing, clapping or any other exalting activity.

God also loves praise because it directs your focus completely on Him, not on your issues. When you praise your circumstances don't exist. Your situations are forgotten. Your needs or concerns are set aside. During praise, you and God experience spiritual intimacy.

II. Know your vision

And the men of Israel said, have ye seen this man that is come up? Surely to defy Israel is he come up: and it shall be, that the man who killeth him, the king will enrich him with great riches, and will give him his daughter, and make his father's house free in Israel.

–1 Samuel 17:25[KJV]

Knowing what you're pursuing is another critical step. Sadly, many people end up exiting this world without ever answering their calling. This cannot, and will not, be you. If you hope to elevate above where you are currently, you must define your end result. What you're striving to accomplish? Success is not possible without knowing your objective. Before he fought Goliath, David knew what he was fighting for.

> Upon arriving to the Israelite camp, David inquires of the men around him the reward for defeating Goliath. The men respond, "The king will enrich him with great riches, and will give him his daughter, and make his father's house free in Israel" (1 Samuel 17:25[KJV]).

The reward is significantly greater than most people realize. Defeating Goliath meant financial security, acceptance into the royal family and David's family's release from taxation. Could you imagine the motivation this gave the young man? An abundance of wealth. Marriage. Family exempted from debt.

God has great rewards waiting for you too; yet, you must know what you're pursuing after. What do you want in life? What has God put in your spirit, heart, and mind to achieve? What do you see when you close your eyes?

Knowing your goal creates momentum, surety. It also repels distractions. People without a defined goal or a specific direction often fail. Proverbs 29:18[KJV] says, "Where there is no vision [goal, purpose and direction], the people perish …" If you're to achieve your vision, define what it is and commit to going after it. Success cannot occur without a defined objective and a commitment to obtain it.

Three Divine Rules to Setting Up Your Vision

1. **Inquire of God for your vision:** God's perfect will dominates any of our personal agendas. If you have trouble determining what your vision is, inquire God about it. Hebrews 11:6[KJV] says, " …he is a rewarder of them that diligently seek him." The reward then is the purpose or vision He has for you. Furthermore, ask Him what He'd like you to pursue. Have a mind to substitute your agenda for His. He will then help you identify the path you're to follow. Proverbs 37:23[KJV] informs, "The steps of a good man are ordered by the LORD: and he delighteth [delights] in his way." Become inquisitive about your future.
2. **Be specific:** Vague or ambiguous goals do not lead to achievement. Thus, all visions must have clarity. Many

people often generalize their goals or desires, but have no specific outline or action plan. "*I want to be financially independent*" ... "*I want to get married*" ... "*I want to help others* ..." And so on. Although they have an idea of their desires, they have no clear avenues to fulfillment or attainment.

Clarification reveals the actions or next moves you should take. It gives details and helps answers the five Ws': who, what, when, why and where. Too much valuable time has been spent on unproductive activities due to unclear visions. To assist in this endeavor, Habakkuk 2:2[KJV] directs, "Write the vision, and <u>make it plain</u> upon tables, that <u>he may run that readeth it</u>."

Making the vision or goal plain, as the scriptures states, reveals the importance of clarity. The "*he may run that readeth it*" equates to the person, or persons, that will help in your achievement. If your help, or team, cannot determine clearly where you're headed, you will become stagnate. Stagnation then becomes another obstacle that you'd need to overcome. Make sure your vision or goal is clear!

3. **Write down your vision:** Writing down your vision builds commitment. It's equivalent to signing your signature to a contract. Writing down your goals also creates an understanding between you and your destiny.

Nehemiah 9:38[NIV] relays, "In view of all this, we are making a binding agreement, putting it in writing ..."

Too often we keep our visions in our minds and attempt to make them tangible from memory. This causes a problem. We're inundated daily by personal and professional demands. We then forget, or set aside our goals, dreams and purpose. Writing down your vision increases its importance in the hierarchy of priorities.

An unwritten vision is merely a powerless thought. If you desire to walk in the power of your future, you must commit to writing down your plans. Show God how serious about your vision or purpose you are by implementing this activity.

III. Operate in the Power of Faith

David said to Saul, "Let no one lose heart on account of this Philistine; your servant will go and fight him".

–1 Samuel 17:32[NIV]

David's unwavering faith in God was instrumental to his success. Faith is unequivocally necessary in everything you do. It is the cornerstone of achievement and the building block of destiny. Hebrews 11:1[KJV] reminds, "faith is the substance of things hoped for, the evidence of things not seen." Every goal, vision or purpose you seek to achieve requires faith. The absence of faith hinders the next dimension to which you're entitled.

As discussed in the Strategy of David, a relationship with God is the foundation of faith. Since David had a strong relationship with Him, he had no doubts about the outcome of the fight. He knew he would have victory. David's confidence shows us that **great faith trumps great opposition**.

Sadly, many men and women desire to operate in promise, or pursue a dream, but lack faith. As a result, they remain despondent or non-responsive to opportunities. God gives them vision for entrepreneurship, but they opt to be a career employee. God drops purpose in their heart, but they rather live in the concentration camps of average. God gives them the opportunity to excel in their passion, but they refuse to give up excuses and alibis. God reveals the missing piece to their happiness, but they continue to accept grief or joylessness. God desires to place them in the palace of greatness, but they prefer the shabbiness of mediocrity.

If you find yourself connected to any of these groups of people, it's time to separate yourself. 2 Corinthians 6:17[NIV] commands, " ...come out from them and be separate, says the Lord ..." Separating yourself from people without vision or purpose lessens their pull on you.

If you wrestle with walking and living in faith, perhaps the fault is not yours to bear. Maybe you lack understanding about what faith is, how it's gained or how it's used. This is common. To use faith effectively, an individual must understand what faith is and how it works.

So what is Faith?

Faith is, "Complete trust or confidence in someone or something." According to Hebrews 11:1[KJV] it is "the substance of things hoped for, the evidence of things not seen."

Essentially, faith is seeing the achievement or end result of your vision before it happens. Amidst strong opposition, your faith sees you as victorious. During the moments of grief, your faith unveils a future of joy and happiness. When overwhelmed by personal and professional challenges, your faith shows you standing triumphantly over your giants.

> No one believed in David. When he told King Saul that he would fight Goliath, the men couldn't fathom his victory. Rather than see David as the solution to their problem, the men saw an inexperienced boy without combat training. Equally insulting, the king discredited young David by saying, "You are not able to go out against this Philistine and fight him; you are only a young man, and he has been a warrior from his youth" (1 Samuel 17:33[NIV]).

In the presence of adverse circumstances, people cannot see who you truly are, nor perceive the value you have. Their preconceived notions about your ability often blind them to the faith you have. As a result, they often judge you prematurely.

Discounting you causes people not to consider an important fact: You are God's response to the oppositions they face. Your hellacious trials helped build your faith and qualified you for these present challenges. You were designed, crafted and forged for the obstacles that demand your surrender.

No one but God knows your depth. He often disguises the greater side of you until the moment requires revealing. If David had listened to the men, and accepted their words in his heart as truth, he would have given up. He would've forfeited the vision and destiny God had for him. Incredibly, David's rejection of the king's and his men's words teach us a valuable lesson: having faith and knowing who you are deflect other people's opinions or low perceptions of you. Nothing the men said impacted David. He had his mind, heart and spirit set on the task before him. You too should be as he.

You must understand that God purposed you to be great, successful, unstoppable, healed and delivered. If your challenges have caused your faith to wither, or you do not know how to strengthen your faith, the following four exercises will assist you.

Four Exercises to Build and Strengthen Your Faith

Faith is a spiritual muscle. When God created you, He placed a measure of faith in your spirit to help you achieve incredible heights in your life. In Romans 12:4[KJV], the scriptures says, " … God has dealt [given] to every man the measure of faith." The challenge then is not that you're faithless; rather the amount you have needs further developing and strengthening. And as with any muscle, such strengthening and developing can only occur through exercise. The following are four exercises you can use to build your faith.

1. **Immerse yourself in study**: Daily study of God's Word, as well as studying the prerequisites of your purpose or vision, is critical. Studying God's Word opens the receptors of your spirit and awakens your mind for enlightenment. Vast study also reveals the amount of time, energy, resources and sacrifices necessary for your

achievement. In 2 Timothy 2:15KJV Paul reminds, "study to show yourself approved." Approved for what? God approves individuals to handle His vision and purpose for their lives based on proper study habits.

If you strive for entrepreneurship, for example, how can you become a successful entrepreneur if you don't study your customers, economic conditions, your competition, and market trends? How can you get delivered if you don't study the Word of God and the examples of others who also received deliverance? How do you walk in your future without studying the requirements of your next level? Accomplishments fail to exist without adequate study habits.

2. **Adopt a vision-centered mindset:** Success at any level, or dimension, usually stands at the border of the toughest times in our lives. Rather than press onward, many people grow fatigue and then give in to defeat prematurely. This is an unacceptable practice for those on the path to great achievements.

   Your mind is an incredible and valuable asset. It produces great ideas, projects big dreams, safeguards imagination and often determines the outcome of each desire. Furthermore, it is the place where battles are either won or loss.

   A mind disciplined and focused on vision is the most powerful weapon in your arsenal. It has the ability to find creative and lucid methods around impossibility. Additionally, it's the catalyst to helping you see possibility in perceivably hopeless moments. Unfortunately, when your mind becomes undisciplined, or contaminated with fear, intimidation, doubt and excuses, it becomes the most powerful weapon in your enemy's arsenal. Satan's greatest strategy is to destroy you through unproductive, disempowering and destructive thinking. This solidifies the importance of study, as it keeps your mind focused and aligned with purpose.

Fortunately, a mind centered on vision wards off distractions. Your vision, then, acts as a protective barrier, or shield, from the infiltration of mental attacks. Exchange mind-numbing activities, relationships with purposeless people and disempowering thoughts with connections that will improve, advance and enhance you. Reject discouragement. Defy doubt. Oppose negativity. Limit unproductive activities. Choose to adopt a vision-centered mindset. Proverbs 4:25[NIV] says, "Let your eyes look straight ahead; fix your gaze directly before you." Looking straight ahead, as the scripture says, requires a mind centered on vision. Vision centricity upsets the enemy!

3. **Take action**: Adequate study and the adoption of a vision-centered mindset are two key faith-strengthening exercises. Another activity that will help strengthen your faith is action.

Action ties together your study and your mental development. It solidifies your understanding and ensures the sustainability of your vision-centered focus. Without action, nothing can happen. James 2:26NKJV affirms, "For as the body without the spirit is dead, so faith without works [action] is dead also."

Your desires, goals, and vision require concerted effort, or action. Consider your own purpose or desires, and then ask yourself this question: "Can I achieve my next level without taking action?" If you answer "no" then make a plan to take action today. Don't wait any longer because procrastination is an enemy to your destiny. Proverbs 13:4NKJV states, "The soul of a lazy man desires, and has nothing; but the soul of the diligent shall be made rich." Action, according to the scripture, ensures achievement and advancement.

4. **Reject temptation:** The road toward purpose and destiny is filled with distractions, feelings of giving in, thoughts of taking shortcuts and many other purpose-hindering issues. During your pursuit of vision or purpose, tough times may tempt you to stop your progress or sway you away from your desires. You must reject such temptations, despite how strong.

   In 1 Corinthians 10:13KJV Apostle Paul says, "There hath no temptation taken you but such as is common to man: but God is faithful, who will not suffer you to be tempted above that ye are able; but will with the temptation also make a way to escape, that ye may be able to bear *it*." What is the scripture saying?

Every person has experienced, or currently experiences, temptation. Yet, although the temptation may seem overwhelming, God has given you the ability to overcome it, and the power not to engage it. No matter the form it takes, your commitment to vision has to be stronger than the temptation. The escape, then, becomes your unshakable devotion to destiny.

One may ask, "Why does temptation exist?"

It's important to understand the motive of temptation. Its primary focus is to distract you from living the life God has for you. The enemy loves sending temptation your way because he knows something about you: when focused you're a dangerous individual and have the power to break his control and influence over people. If he can keep you distracted, you'll never fulfill the ideas, pursue your purpose or commit to the vision God gave you. Do not let his enticements cause you to deviate from God's plan for your life, despite the struggle. In Romans 7:21[KJV], Paul states, " ...when I would do good, evil [temptation] is present with me." When the opportunity of temptation arises, remember your future. Nothing is worth your destiny!

> Rejecting temptation says, "My future is too important for me to give in to this temporary moment!" "I've gone through too much not to receive the blessings God has for me!" "I cannot and will not let my struggle keep me away from the quality of life I deserve." "I refuse to live another moment under my potential."
>
> You have too much to offer this world—your family—your Lord—to let something as cunning as temptation overtake you. Your struggle or distraction is not as strong as you believe. When it seems too difficult to overcome, be reminded of Isaiah 59:19[KJV]: "When the enemy comes in like a flood, the Spirit of the Lord shall lift up a standard against him." Keep in mind that you are greater than the pull of temptation.

God has great wonders in store for you. In Ephesians 3:20[KJV], God affirms you can have "exceedingly abundantly above all you ask or think, according to the power that worketh in us." What is this power that works in you? Faith! Faith is the key to turning every thought, inclination, purpose or vision into its tangible and manifested forms. Faith divides greatness from mediocrity and excellence from average. Build and strengthen your faith and expect great changes to happen in your life.

IV. Use the Momentum of Your Past Victories:

But David said to Saul, "Your servant used to keep his father's sheep, and when a lion or a bear came and took a lamb out of the flock, I went out after it and struck it, and delivered *the lamb* from its mouth; and when it arose against me, I caught *it* by its beard, and struck and killed it. Your servant has killed both lion and bear; and this uncircumcised Philistine will be like one of them, seeing he has defied the armies of the living God."

–1 Samuel 17:35-36[KJV]

Your past is filled with many battles. Some may have left you emotionally scarred and stripped of happiness, while others may have nearly destroyed you financially, spiritually or physically. But by God's grace you still stand—victoriously.

Looking back over your life, have you ever wondered why you had to undergo the hardships, or experience the crippling moments of your past? Ever found yourself saying, "Why me, Lord?"

God used your past as divine training for your purpose. Every hurt, loss or obstacle you ever experienced was designed to strengthen and prepare you for the giant you now face. Psalms 119:71[NIV] says, "It was good for me to be afflicted [hurt, challenged] so that I might learn your decrees [principles, understanding]." The principle, or understanding, then is the knowledge that you are a conqueror.

> Standing before King Saul, David summarizes his qualifications; his past victories. He says with confidence, "Your servant used to keep his father's sheep, and <u>when a lion and a bear came and took a lamb</u> out of the flock, <u>I went out after it and struck it</u>, and delivered *the lamb* from its mouth; and when it arose against me, I caught *it* by

> its beard, and struck and killed it. Your servant has killed both lion and bear ..." (1 Samuel 17:34-36[KJV])

God has been with you through your past trials. As He did with David, He has helped you overcome every situation that nearly killed you spiritually, financially, emotionally or physically. Helping you through the valley of affliction (even when you didn't feel Him) was to build up your confidence—to spark the flame of courage inside you—for this moment.

Whereas many people see their past as a hindrance, you should see yours differently. Your past challenges were the boot camp to help prepare you for your current giant. David's past victories, for example, would not allow him to see Goliath as a champion. Rather, he saw the embodiment of two enemies he had already defeated: a lion and a bear. This revelation gave David the gall to speak and act confidently in an atmosphere of doubt and fear.

After reading the above paragraph, you may ask, "How did Goliath embody a lion and a bear?"

Lions often assert their dominance and spark fear through a thunderous roar. Bears, on the other hand, often provoke intimidation by standing on their hind legs. When standing, their height can range between six and eleven feet.

Considering the nature of the lion and the bear, David saw Goliath nothing more than a compound of these two animals. Goliath's forty-day rant, for example, was equivalent to a lion's roar. Each day he roared mightily with insults and mockery, sparking fear in Israel. His height made him equivalent to a nine-foot bear. Since Goliath represented two beasts David had already defeated, he had no reason to be afraid.

Now look at your Goliath. You may notice that your current giant is merely the embodiment of enemies you've already defeated. The present circumstance may appear differently than those of your past, but their nature is the same. You've already beat inadequacy. You already defeated struggle. You've already conquered depression. You've already overcome hurt. You've kicked addiction. Your obstacle then is adverse challenges partnering against you—to force you into submission. They will not prevail! God is allowing these joined forces to push you—to give you the opportunity to turn those who ever doubted you into believers. Romans 8:28[KJV] reminds, "And we know that all things work together for good to them that love God, to them who are the called according to his purpose."

To get you to the next dimension of greatness, the heartache had to happen. The emotional attack had to happen. The disappointment had to happen. The financial crisis had to happen. The betrayal had to happen. The loss had to happen. The sickness had to happen. Now summon your greatness and reveal the power of God in you. Use the momentum of your past victories to stand victoriously over your giant.

V. Remove the Weight

So Saul clothed David with his armor, and he put a bronze helmet on his head; he also clothed him with a coat of mail [armor]. David fastened [attached] his sword to his armor and tried to walk, for he had not tested [approved] *them*. And David said to Saul, "I cannot walk with these, for I have not tested [approved] *them*." So <u>David took them off</u>".

–1 Samuel 17:30-39[NKJV], emphasis added

We often pursue our vision while carrying unnecessary weight. The responsibility of others, living up to people's expectations and many other "anchors" make progress strenuous. As a result, we become overwhelmed, stressed out and unmotivated. Hebrews 12:1[KJV] directs us to, "lay aside every weight, and the sin which doth so easily beset [entangle] us."

The weight or pressure we often carry either is oppression from people, unhealthy attachments or distractions. Any of these make operating in purpose and vision difficult. Thus, you must remove the weight, or set aside the hindrances, to ensure your future. You cannot expect to enter your destiny while carrying needless baggage. Saul's perceivably kind act, for example, would have been detrimental to David's success.

Saul's placing his armor on David would appear a noble action, but it was against God's desire. God never intended David to go into battle (or into his destiny), with someone else's weight on him. Despite how generous the gesture, Saul's armor would have hindered David's victory. How is this?

King Saul's armor was tailored to his height and size. As the tallest Israelite, his armor would not have fitted David's boyish frame comfortably (1 Samuel 9:2). If David had engaged Goliath while wearing the king's armor, he may have met an unfortunate demise.

As you examine your own life, answer the following questions. Whose weight are you carrying? How many times have you gone after your dream while carrying the burdens of family and friends? Why are you carrying your past with you? How many times were you hindered by the cares or affairs of others?

God neither intended David nor you to face Goliath with anyone else's armor or weight. The future He has for you is designed specifically for you; no one else. This may seem selfish, but be assured it isn't. 1 Peter 4:10[NLT] says, "God has given each person a gift from His variety of spiritual gifts." Each individual then is personally responsible for his or her own journey. This includes family, friends, associates and other constituents that may overwhelm you.

If you're going to progress in your life, you must take off the weight. Remove the burdens of failed relationships. Shake off the disappointment of missed opportunities. Throw off the worry of what's to come. Release yourself from other people's expectations. Starting today let no one or anything keep you bound or weighed down.

VI. Gather Necessary Resources

Then he took his staff in his hand; and he chose for himself five smooth stones from the brook, and put them in a shepherd's bag, in a pouch which he had, and his sling was in his hand.

–1 Samuel 17:40[NKJV]

Defeating your Goliath requires gathering and leveraging key resources. These resources may include creating partnerships with experts in their fields of study, selecting a team of purpose-driven individuals, developing and implementing a business plan, or acquiring certain education. Collecting the right resources will result in a triumphant victory over your opposition.

David's choice of weapons was merely a collection of vital resources. Each weapon he chose served a specific purpose.

The Sling

Slings were dangerous weapons and widely used in ancient warfare. Their accuracy, effectiveness and compartmentalization made them attractive. Warriors of ancient times would use slings to defeat enemies within close proximity. Light and easy to use, they were the perfect weapon.

For your battle think of slings as leveraging tools—devices, or people that can help you. While face-to-face with your Goliath, you should think about whom or what you can leverage. Think about whom or what can support your ideas.

The Smooth Stones

The Bible does not use adjectives without reason. In the scripture, David chooses five smooth stones from the brook. Why did he choose smooth stones instead of plain rocks?

Before we address this question, it's important to note the following: stones are not naturally smooth. They're often jagged, rough. Stones are made smooth by erosion—"the process by which something is eroded or worn away by natural sources such as water, wind or ice." The water from the brook, in this case, caused the stones' smooth surface. Science then confirms that smooth stones (when flung) will travel at a higher velocity than at the rate of regular stones. This will result in a greater and more controlled impact.

In relation to your life, the smooth stones are the ammunition you need to knock down your giant. They represent the connections and relationships with individuals whose mindsets and attitudes had undergone the "erosion by the brook of life." They have successfully undergone hardships to help you stand victorious—successful.

Once you select your smooth stones, use your sling to hurl them at the head of your giant. Here's something important to remember. Your giant cannot fall without your smooth stones. Combined with your sling, no giant stands a chance.

VII. Speak Your Victory into Existence

Then David said to the Philistine [Goliath], "You come to me with a sword, with a spear, and with a javelin. But I come to you in the name of the LORD of hosts, the God of the armies of Israel, whom you have defied. This day the LORD will deliver you into my hand, and I will strike you and take your head from you. And this day I will give the carcasses [corpses] of the camp of the Philistines to the birds of the air and the wild beasts [animals] of the earth, that all the earth may know that there is a God in Israel. Then all this assembly shall know that the LORD does not save with sword and spear; for the battle *is* the LORD's, and He will give you into our hands"

–1 Samuel 17:45-47[NKJV], emphasis added

A strong part of your strategic plan is to prophesy, or dictate, your victory. Your situation, or circumstance, has been terrorizing, demeaning and belittling you far too long. It's been letting you know how miniscule or incapable you are. Now use the authority God gave you to speak back to your Goliath.

Goliath spoke very disrespectfully to David, envisioning a quick win over the young man: He says, "Am I a dog that you come at me with sticks?" ... "Come here ... and I'll give your flesh to the birds and the wild animals!" (1 Samuel 17:42-44[NIV])

Unmoved by Goliath's death threats, David responds, "This day the LORD will deliver you into my hand, and I will strike you and take your head from you."

You can no longer allow your situations or circumstances make you feel inadequate. You can no longer let hardships determine your life. You are greater and far more phenomenal than the giant by whom you've become taunted. Look at your adversity and let it know about its imminent future. Let it know that, "This day the LORD will deliver you into my hand, and I will strike you and take your head from you."

Take the dare and tell debt and financial destitution that their time has come to an end. Advise brokenness, loneliness and sadness about their impending replacement with happiness and joy. Instruct illness to vacate the premises of your mind and body effective immediately.

God has given you the authority to talk your victory into existence. Mark 11:23[KJV] empowers, " ...That whosoever shall say unto this mountain [hardship, obstacle or challenge], be thou [you] removed, and be thou [you] cast into the sea; and shall not doubt in his heart, but shall believe that those things which he saith [says] shall come to pass; he shall have whatsoever he saith [says]." (Emphasis added)

Part of your victory stems from the words you bring out your mouth. As someone created in God's image, you have the ability to actualize anything you believe and say. Romans

4:17KJV advises us to " ...calleth [call] those things which be not as though they were."

The scripture intimates vital information. If you believe and say you're victorious, you'll become victorious. If you believe and say you're defeated, you'll become defeated. Essentially, you manifest the result of your situation through the power of your lips. Luke 6:45KJV affirms, " ...for of the abundance of his heart the mouth speaketh." The scripture reveals your heart then as the breeding ground from which your deepest feelings are spoken.

If you ever spoke negatively about your abilities, bring these conversations to an end. If you ever said you couldn't do something, refuse to say it ever again. You already have enough people and circumstances desiring your defeat. No need to join them. Instead, talk back to your Goliath and remind it of its unfortunate future. Speak your victory into existence. Get good at saying, "I will succeed!" "I will win!" "I will conquer!"

VIII. Concentrate Your Focus and Resources

So it was, when the Philistine arose and came and drew near to meet David, that David hurried and ran toward the army to meet the Philistine. Then David put his hand in his bag and took out a stone; and he slung *it* and struck the Philistine in his forehead, so that the stone sank into his forehead, and he [Goliath] fell on his face to the earth [ground]. So David prevailed over the Philistine with a sling and a stone, and struck the Philistine and killed him.

–1 Samuel 17:48-50NKJV, emphasis added

Every Goliath has a weakness. Once you identify it, channel all your energy and resources on it. This requires unbreakable focus.

> Facing Goliath, David spots a weakness on the giant, undiscovered by King Saul and the men of Israel: his forehead. Eyes and mind set on his target, he hurls a smooth stone (or one of his resources), at the mark. The undefeatable giant falls (1 Samuel 17:48-50).

David's ability to identify and attack Goliath's weakness reveals an important point: only aim for and attack the head of your issue; not the body. King Saul was intimidated and overwhelmed because he focused on the "body" of Goliath. To avoid being intimidated, concentrate all your energy, resources and effort on the forehead of your circumstance.

At this stage in your strategy, you have the power to make your giant fall. Feelings of inadequacy and insignificance must fall. Financial hardships must fall. The sickness in your body must fall. Your addiction must fall. Unhappiness must fall. Heartache must fall. Any circumstance or "giant" that has hindered you must, and will, fall. This is only made possible by implementing and executing the strategy of David.

The Strategy of David

I. **Build and Maintain a Relationship with God**
II. **Know Your Vision**
III. **Operate in the Power of Faith**

IV. **Use the Momentum of Your Past Victories**

V. **Remove the Weight**

VI. **Gather Necessary Resources**

VII. **Speak Your Victory into Existence**

VIII. **Concentrate Your Focus and Resources**

After This

Therefore David ran and stood over the Philistine, took his [Goliath's] sword and drew it out of its sheath and killed him, and cut off his head with it. And when the Philistines saw that their champion was dead, they fled. Now the men of Israel and Judah arose and shouted, and pursued the Philistines as far as the entrance of the valley and to the gates of Ekron.

–1 Samuel 17:51-52[KJV], emphasis added

Defeating your Goliath will open many doors for you. More doors than you ever thought possible. If your giant is financial hardship, expect a life of financial freedom. If it's overcoming broken heartedness, expect a relationship of appreciation and devotion. If your Goliath is breaking the cycle of sickness or addictions, expect to be healed or delivered. Despite the type of Goliath you face, expect favorable results.

Although your victory will open doors to a new life, it will also do something else extraordinary: inspire and empower others to do the same, or greater.

David's defeat over Goliath not only benefited him, but it resuscitated hope and courage in the once fearful men of Israel. "And when the Philistines saw that their champion was dead, they fled. Now the men of Israel and Judah arose and shouted, and pursued the Philistines ..." This is magnificent. Recall earlier how afraid and hopeless the king and his men were in Goliath's presence. After witnessing David's victory, they regained strength and confidence.

Once you kill your giant, you will empower many individuals to pursue their own vision, dream, desire or purpose. Your victory will cause family, friends, constituents and acquaintances to awaken their own David. Consider how the actions of a child helped his father activate his David.

Pushed Forward

As my one-year-old child rests his head on my chest, his body strangely grows warm. He didn't show any signs of illness earlier. My wife and I then take his temperature—a life-threatening 103.2 degrees. In a panic, we immediately rush him to the hospital.

Upon arriving to the emergency room, the nurse takes my son's temperature: an alarming 104.7 degrees. The medical staff quickly undresses him and implements what I call "operation cool down."

My wife and I watch the staff poke and prod our child. He cries uncontrollably. My eyes tear up as I think about the other madness I had going on: financial challenges, my wife's frequent battle with her illness and overwhelming workplace demands. On the brink of breakdown, I wonder if this was God's payback for something I had done in my life. I repent. I pray. I repent again ...

After running several tests, the doctors discover my son to have a viral infection and then admit him to pediatric care. Holding my little man in her arms, my wife says, "I'll stay with him. You go home and get some rest." Saddened by my child's condition, I stare at my exhausted son. "Okay," I respond, struggling to keep from crying. Upon leaving my child's hospital room, I close the door. Tears stream uncontrollably down my face...sleep never happens.

The day after would strangely change my attitude. God must have been busy. After leaving work, I return to the hospital to see my child and to relieve my wife. I'm sure she needed to rest. Upon entering the room, I see a phenomenal sight: my wife and child laughing and playing. My son oddly appears healthy, oblivious to the IV in his arm. I pick him up, kiss his cheek. He stares back at me, smiling as if nothing had happened. Suddenly, the chains of worry snap. If my child could laugh after experiencing excruciating pain and restlessness, I thought; I had to press forward for him. His strength gave me the strength I needed to move on. He helped me to awaken my David.

Whereas my child's victory over his health condition pushed me to press onward, you will do the same for others. Countless individuals are depending on your victory. Philippians 2:3-4NIV urges us to, "Do nothing out of selfish ambition or vain conceit. Rather, in humility value others above yourselves, not looking to your own interests but each of you to the interests of the others."

Because of your victory, people will break the control of addictions. Because of your victory, people will acquire financial independence. Because of your victory, people will break the chains of heartache and sickness. Because of your victory, generational curses will become generational promises. Because of your victory, people will pursue happiness, purpose or vision. Because of your victory, confidence in God (and personal ability) will be restored. That said, you should think of your victory as a gift.

Your Victory is a Gift

Each of you should use whatever gift you have received to serve others, as faithful stewards of God's grace in its various forms.

–1 Peter 4:10NIV

Your victory is a gift of empowerment and hope. In essence this makes you a giver—an unselfish person who God sees worthy of additional blessings. The return to a giver is loftier than someone who always receives. Luke 6:38KJV says, "Give, and it shall be given unto you; good measure, pressed down, and shaken together, and running over, shall men give into your bosom …" Proverbs 11:24NIV states, "One person gives freely, yet gains even more; another withholds unduly, but comes to poverty."

Everyone who becomes empowered by your victory will be indebted to you. Their payback may not be as you expect. Some may say "thanks" and then walk away, not to ever be heard from again. That's fine. Some may reward you financially, invest in your vision, or even request a partnership with you. That's great. Some may hire you because you have the talent and ability to increase their success tenfold. That's outstanding. There is, however, a select few God will use to create more opportunities for you. This is astounding and most desirable.

David's defeat over Goliath resolved King Saul's problem. Although David initially expected to marry the king's daughter, acquire wealth and set his family free from taxation, he received something vastly more valuable. In return for his "gift," King Saul rewarded David with a leadership role, royal connections and residency within the palace (1 Samuel 18:1-5). This opportunity far exceeded the rewards he originally sought after. How is this? There are a few reasons.

1. A place in the king's palace meant David would have access to the king and his wisdom. Through this opportunity, David would learn how to speak and act wisely. He would also learn firsthand about politics and other kingly duties.
2. While in the palace David would develop royal relationships. For example, 1 Samuel 18:1 reveals the brotherly relationship he develops with King Saul's son, Jonathan. From this relationship, David would gain favor and support.
3. David would assume responsibility over the king's men. This leadership role would further increase David's

> leadership effectiveness, strategic thinking and expand his knowledge of military etiquette.

God had a purpose for placing David in the palace. Since David's true destiny was to become king, he had to learn both acceptable and unacceptable practices from Saul. An effective leader learns from others' successes and mistakes.

God has a similar plan for you. As the King of kings, He desires to take you from the fields of complacency and mediocrity to the palace of excellence and longevity. He desires to place you before people with affluence, influence and position to help you succeed. The next phase of your life requires the skills and connections that you will gain from these relationships.

If God can take an unknown teenager with lowly beginnings (and who was often doubted by family and others), what do you think He'll do for you? More than you think. Ezekiel 34:26[NIV] says, "I [God] will make them and the places surrounding my hill a blessing. I will send down showers in season; there will be showers of blessing." Are you in need of blessings?

Once you defeat your Goliath, get ready for the showers of happiness, favor and success. Get ready for deliverance and healing. Get excited because God is preparing you for the next stage of excellence. The time has come for you to claim everything that's rightfully yours. Deuteronomy 11:24[NIV] says, "Every place where you set your foot will be yours …" Therefore, start walking in your calling. Become ecstatic about your purpose.

Your Now is not Where You Belong

"For I know the plans I have for you," declares the LORD, "plans to prosper you and not to harm you, plans to give you hope and a future."

–Jeremiah 29:11[NIV]

As a child of God, you are a royal individual. Despite all you have done, or had undergone, God has set His affections on you. He desires to take you from where you are to where you belong. This place is in His will and His purpose. If you are unaware of your value to Him, consider 1 Peter 2:9[NIV]. The scripture reminds, "But you are a chosen people, a royal priesthood, a holy nation, God's special possession, that you may declare the praises of him who called you out of darkness into his wonderful light."

Being chosen by God gives you the right to be successful; the right to be healed; the right to be delivered; and the right to be happy. As royalty and God's special possession, you have the power to attain everything you have in your spirit. Notice, however, the latter part of the scripture: " …declare the praises of Him who called you out of darkness into his wonderful light."

Before you can walk in your purpose, God has to bring you out of the darkness of doubt; bring you out of darkness of disbelief; bring you out of the darkness of unhappiness; and bring you out of the darkness of ungodly thinking. You may ask, "How would I know when I am out of darkness?"

You are removed from darkness once you come into the understanding or the "light" of His mind, the "light" of His will, the "light" of His desire, and the "light" of His divine order.

Once you understand God's will for your life, you're operating in the "light." Thus, a major part of God's will is for you to defeat your giant. Do not wait another moment.

Patience vs. Procrastination

...But he who follow empty pursuits will have poverty in plenty.
–Proverbs 28:19^NASB

Your time and life are too valuable not to achieve the blessings God has for you. You cannot spend another moment, day, week, month or year wondering if defeating your giant is possible. It is. Your struggle or challenge has been defeated before. Ecclesiastes 1:9^KJV tells, " ...there's no new thing under the sun." To elaborate, every obstacle set before you have been overcome by someone else.

Although God has given each person the power to claim his or her victory, many will refuse to move forward. Instead they might say, "I'm waiting on God's direction." Waiting on God is critical to your future, but this statement often is an excuse. 2 Peter 1:3^NIV accounts, "<u>His divine power has given us everything</u> we need for a godly life through our knowledge of Him who called us by His own glory and goodness."

If God has already given us everything we need, why then wait? Why then put off the tasks or actions necessary for your future? Unfortunately, procrastination is the culprit.

Many people confuse patience with procrastination. Despite popular belief, these two words are very different. The following definitions will give you clarity and differentiation between them.

The definition of patience is, "the quality of being patient, as the bearing of provocation, annoyance, misfortune, or pain, without complaint, loss of temper, irritation, or the like." In Hebrew the word patience (qavah) means "to wait for, to look for, to hope, or to expect." In Greek, patience (hypomenō) means, "to remain, to abide, to preserver, to endure, or to bear bravely and calmly."

Patience, then, from both a biblical and life perspective means, "waiting for, looking and hoping for, persevering, enduring, expecting, bearing, remaining and abiding without complaint or loss of temper" for God's direction. Most people who often operate in patience are found seeking God for their purpose or vision. They are collaborating with others, collecting resources, or waiting for God to direct their next steps. This is patience.

Procrastination, on the other hand, is the mindset and spirit in which most people operate. It's defined as, "the act or habit of procrastinating, or putting off or delaying, especially something requiring immediate attention." In Hebrew, procrastination (achar) means, "to put off, delay, remain behind, and hinder." Similarly in Greek, procrastination (anavoli) means, "the action of delaying or postponing something." Individuals who operate in the spirit of procrastination usually have vision, purpose or destiny, but refuse to take action. Like King Saul and the men of Israel, when faced with Goliath, they find reasons not to press forward.

After reviewing the two definitions, where do you stand? Are you operating in the spirit of patience or procrastination? If you're truly operating in patience, continue to seek God's direction and His purpose for your life. He will reveal them to you.

If, however, you're under the duress of procrastination, ask yourself why? What about your future causes reluctance? What's keeping you from moving forward? Answering honestly will help you and God clear a pathway for your tomorrow. Remember, your blessings will only follow after identifying your Goliath; activating your David; and strategizing your victory. Only after this will you walk in power and defeat your Goliath. Decide today to breach the contract with mediocrity and engage a new partnership with destiny.

Words from the Author

This book was written with you in mind; the individual with the potential to achieve greatness and happiness.

The power to acquire all you desire rests within you. You have the innate ability to kill any giant that stands in your way. Once you understand how incredible you truly are, you'll walk amongst the great Goliath killers. You will no longer wrestle with whether you can succeed, be healed, get delivered or break generational curses because you can.

If this book has touched you positively; has given you insight; has inspired you; or has enlightened you in any way, please share it with someone else. This day and age people need empowerment, inspiration and direction. Many people are stagnated or beaten right now because they don't know how to defeat their Goliath. You now have the tools and the power to help them. Hebrews 13:16 NIV says, "…do not forget to do good and to share with others, for with such sacrifices God is pleased."

Sharing information or giving an action plan such as this is one of your divine assignments. That being said, think about the family members, friends, coworkers, acquaintances or constituents who could use this for their own lives. Jot down their names and put next to each name the date which you will send him, her or them a copy.

Once you have your list of people to bless, go to your favorite online bookstore, or visit www.EllardThomas.com or www.Defeating-Goliath.com, to order Defeating Goliath for them. On the websites you will discover more about the author, have the chance to sign up for the Barrier Breaker newsletter, order other inspiring books such as the must-have **Moving Forward, Courageously: Seven Secrets to Restoring Love, Money and Happiness in Your Life**, and receive updates on upcoming books, seminars and conferences. The ultimate goal is to help you achieve the results you desire in your life.

If you do not have the financial means to purchase Defeating Goliath as a gift for others, but you'd like to spread the word, this is also welcomed. You may blog about how the book has helped you; tweet your feelings about it; or send your Facebook friends a message with the websites where they can get it themselves. They will thank you.

Why I Wrote This

I wrote this book as an obedient servant to God. Following the untimely death of my mother (and after consecutive hospitalizations of my wife and son), I wanted to quit and do nothing. I questioned my life and had no desire to move on.

A few days following my son's admittance to the hospital, I drove to work depressed. As I walked toward the doors of my workplace, I heard the Holy Spirit say, "Defeating Goliath!" I didn't understand. Perhaps I didn't want to understand. My mother was gone. My wife and son took turns being in the hospital and I was extremely exhausted—emotionally and physically. The Spirit then advised me to study how David defeated the unbeaten giant. From that moment onward, I dedicated every moment, despite emotional turmoil, to complete the work you just read. It was not easy; then again, no worthwhile task is.

God's message is designed to empower, to provoke, to enlighten, to free and to heal people. Everyone needs God and His direction. This kept me going when I started to lose momentum. Psalms 96:3[NKJV] enlightens, "Declare His glory among the nations, His wonders among all peoples." Despite the hardships I had to undergo, I have been truly transformed by this project—you will be too.

Prayerfully, you have become empowered and have made up your mind to become a giant killer. The next words you will read are **A Prayer of Victory** and several scriptures to help advance you in your journey. Thank you for reading and implementing these Goliath-defeating techniques in your life. And remember this before we part. You're too phenomenal, too valuable and too incredible to God, your family and others not to achieve your destiny. You are David!

Many Blessings to you,

Ellard Thomas

Ellard L. Thomas, MBA
www.EllardThomas.com
www.Defeating-Goliath.com
www.Facebook.com/EllardThomas

A Prayer of Victory

(Written for you to recite!)

"Father God, Lord Jesus, I come before you to say thank you for all you have done, what you're doing, and what you're going to do. Although I face some tough challenges in my life, I know you'll bring me through this. You said I am more than a conqueror! Please forgive me for my doubts or disbelief. Open my heart and my mind to Your will. Cleanse me. Help me to walk in my calling. I know I have not done everything right, but I know you are merciful and loving. Please guide me through the darkness of my misunderstanding and bring healing to my heart. I desire you in my life. This day, with your help, I vow to trust in you. I vow to strive toward the higher calling you have for my life. Give me the strength to remove distractions, overcome my past and walk fearlessly in my future. Forgive me for anyone I may have hurt and help me to forgive those who hurt me. Give me strength. Give me wisdom. Give me power. In Jesus name, I pray and declare I am victorious! Thank you Lord!"

Power Scriptures

The Word of God is powerful, sharper than a two-edged sword. Whatever your struggle is, or whatever it is you seek, the Word of God will lead you. The following scriptures were selected to help you become an overcomer, conqueror and a living testimony to help you afoot your destiny.

DELIVERANCE:

- "If we are thrown into the blazing furnace, the God we serve is able to deliver us from it, and he will deliver us from Your Majesty's hand. But even if he does not, we want you to know, Your Majesty, that we will not serve your gods or worship the image of gold you have set up!"

  –Daniel 3: 17-18 NIV

- "And everyone who calls on the name of the LORD will be saved; for on Mount Zion and in Jerusalem there will be deliverance, as the LORD has said, even among the survivors whom the LORD calls."

  –Joel 2:32 NIV

- "Our God is a God who saves; from the Sovereign LORD comes escape from death."

  –Psalms 68:20[NIV]

- "The LORD is my rock, my fortress and my deliverer; my God is my rock, in whom I take refuge, my shield and the horn of my salvation. He is my stronghold, my refuge and my savior—from violent people you save me."

  –2 Samuel 22:2-3[NIV]

FORGIVENESS:

- "For if you forgive men when they sin against you, your heavenly Father will also forgive you. But if you do not forgive men their sins, your Father will not forgive your sins."

  –Matthew 6:14-15[NIV]

- "Bear with each other and forgive one another if any of you has a grievance against someone. Forgive as the Lord forgave you."

  –Colossians 3:13[NIV]

- "Love is patient, love is kind. It does not envy, it does not boast, it is not proud. It does not dishonor others, it is not self-seeking, it is not easily angered, it keeps no record of wrongs. Love does not delight in evil but rejoices with the truth."

  –1 Corinthians 13:4-6[NIV]

- "Do not judge, and you will not be judged. Do not condemn, and you will not be condemned. Forgive, and you will be forgiven."

  –Luke 6:37NIV

HEALING:

- "So do not fear, for I am with you; do not be dismayed, for I am your God. I will strengthen you and help you; I will uphold you with my righteous right hand."

  –Isaiah 41:10NIV

- "He himself bore our sins" in his body on the cross, so that we might die to sins and live for righteousness; "by his wounds you have been healed."

  –1 Peter 2:24NIV

- "Nevertheless, I will bring health and healing to it; I will heal my people and will let them enjoy abundant peace and security."

  –Jeremiah 33:6NIV

- "But he was pierced for our transgressions, he was crushed for our iniquities; the punishment that brought us peace was on him, and by his wounds we are healed."

  –Isaiah 53:5NIV

SUCCESS:

- "Blessed is the one who does not walk in step with the wicked or stand in the way that sinners take or sit in the company of mockers, but whose delight is in the law of the LORD, and who meditates on his law day and night. That person is like a tree planted by streams of water, which yields its fruit in season and whose leaf does not wither – whatever they do prospers."

  –Psalms 1:1-3^NIV

- "What good will it be for someone to gain the whole world, yet forfeit their soul? Or what can anyone give in exchange for their soul?"

  –Matthew 16:26^NIV

- "And my God will meet all your needs according to the riches of his glory in Christ Jesus."

  –Philippians 4:19^NIV

- "You did not choose me, but I chose you and appointed you so that you might go and bear fruit – fruit that will last – and so that whatever you ask in my name the Father will give you."

  –John 15:16^NIV

WEALTH:

- "Honor the LORD with your wealth, with the first fruits of all your crops; then your barns will be filled to overflowing, and your vats will brim over with new wine."

  –Proverbs 3:9-10[NIV]

- "Keep this Book of the Law always on your lips; meditate on it day and night, so that you may be careful to do everything written in it. Then you will be prosperous and successful."

  –Joshua 1:8[NIV]

- "Moreover, when God gives someone wealth and possessions, and the ability to enjoy them, to accept their lot and be happy in their toil—this is a gift of God."

  –Ecclesiastes 5:19[NIV]

- "You may say to yourself, "My power and the strength of my hands have produced this wealth for me." [18] But remember the LORD your God, for it is he who gives you the ability to produce wealth, and so confirms his covenant, which he swore to your ancestors, as it is today."

  –Deuteronomy 8:17-18[NIV]

Acknowledgments

This book could not have happened without the following people touching my life and holding me accountable to moving forward during my darkest moments:

To my Heavenly Father;

I thank you for saving a wretch like me. Without you Jesus, I am nothing. Thank you for choosing me to write this book. Thank you for the experiences, people and resources that contributed to this work's completion. I pray you continue to heal, deliver and save the men and women that need Your love, guidance and direction for their lives.

To my beautiful wife, Kimberly Thomas, and my phenomenal son, Ellard L. Thomas II;

You two are the reasons why I get up every morning. Your strength and love push me to go beyond my own physical, emotional and spiritual limitations. Whenever I think I cannot go any further, you remind me differently. Thank you so much for allowing me to be your husband and father. You are the wind beneath my wings pushing me to greater heights. I love you both so much. Without you I am nothing but an empty vessel.

To my parents Terence Taylor and Vanessa Hunter;

Thank you for life. The start of my achievements occurred when you chose to share affection with one another. Despite any differences we may have had, they were necessary to help me become who I am today. Thank you for every moment we've shared together and the knowledge you gave me. It will never go forgotten. Love you both!

To my siblings Shameka Finister, Christopher Hunter, Eddie Hunter, Betty Hunter, Christopher Coleman and Ki-Von Taylor;

You have impacted me in so many ways. I love you all very much. I pray God continues to cover you and help you reach the destiny He has for you. Without my family, I am nothing more than another man seeking to find his own purpose. Thank you for your love and help in shaping the person I have become. Remember you're too great to settle for anything or anyone. Stay with God and let Him guide you!

To my spiritual fathers and mentors Pastor Gary Hay, Sr., and Pastor Dr. Kevin A. Williams;

Words alone cannot express enough what you two mean to me. Your integrity, commitment to God, devotion to family, fatherly advice and direction, and your selflessness provoke me to become greater and better. God had strategically placed me in your ministries—to sharpen, to strengthen and to shape me. You two are Godsends. Continue in the Faith and keep saving souls. Thank you for being my spiritual fathers. You are truly powerful men of God. I pray God continues to show favor and mercy for you, your family, and your ministries. God bless you both. Thank you very much for teaching and leading me. I am forever in your debt!

To my 'stones' Dr. Erick Pryor, Brad Powell, Tana E. Williams, John Rich, Christina Spencer, Kimberly Reaves, Brenda Hampton, Clifford Seagroves, Drew Seagroves, Dwayne Deloatch, Sharon Pouncy, Hannah Cunningham, Kyle Carver and family, Kiesha Madkins, Benjamin Harris, Jasmine Warren, Travis Burgess, Saeng Palangvanh, Cassandra Boyd, Ann Howerton, Bryce Carter and family, Cory Johnson, Jim Thurston, Sean Fay, Shakeitha Howard, Robin Williams and family, Samuel Miller, Jr., Joshua Gordan, and Malesha Poole;

You believed in the vision of Defeating Goliath when it was merely a concept. Your generosity and your desire to help others have made this a reality. I thank God for placing you in my life and putting it on your heart to support this work. Because of your selflessness and belief, countless people will have the power to defeat their giants. I cannot thank each of you enough. I pray God blesses you and your families. I pray you walk in the strength and power of your calling. I pray the investment you made in the ministry result in favor, abundance, prosperity, healing and anything else you seek from God. Thank you very much for your support!

To my fellow armor bearers F. Maurice Farrow, Josh Garrett, Marcus Witherspoon, Bryce Carter, Kyle Carver and Marquis Jenkins;

Serving with you has been both a joy and pleasure. Continue to advance in your calling and shoot for the stars. I believe in you and expect nothing but greatness from you. Within you is the spirit of excellence. Be unmoved by opposition and remain rooted in God. Continue to support each other and let's impact the world as we had discussed so many times.

Resources

The Holy Bible. New International Version (NIV®). Retrieved from http://www.biblica.com/en-us/the-niv-bible/

The Holy Bible. New King James Version (NKJV) Retrieved from https://www.biblegateway.com/versions/New-King-James-Version-NKJV-Bible/

The Holy Bible. New Living Translation (NLT). Retrieved from https://www.biblegateway.com/versions/New-Living-Translation-NLT-Bible/

The Bible Study Site. (2015). Meaning of Numbers in the Bible. Retrieved from http://www.biblestudy.org/bibleref/meaning-of-numbers-in-bible/8.html

Agape Bible Study. (2015). The Significance of Numbers in Scripture. Retrieved from http://www.agapebiblestudy.com

New American Standard Bible (NASB). The Lockman Foundation. (© 1960, 1962, 1963, 1968, 1971, 1972, 1973, 1975, 1977 & 1995). Retrieved from https://www.bible.com/versions/100-nasb-new-american-standard-bible

The Hebrew-Greek Key Word Study Bible. King James Version. Second Revised Edition. (©1984, 1990 & 2008). AMG International, Inc.

Understanding the Healing Power of Confession. Retrieved from http://www.ignatius.com/promotions/cfe/documents/Forgiven%20web%20pages.pdf

Department of Anthropology. (Abstract 2009). Reward, addiction and emotion regulation systems associated with rejection of love. Retrieved from http://www.ncbi.nlm.nih.gov/pubmed/20445032

Mindtools (2015). Developing Personal Accountability. Taking Responsibility to Get Ahead. Retrieved from http://www.mindtools.com/pages/article/developing-personal-accountability.htm

Fighting Loss and Moving Forward. (2015). You can get through anything. Retrieved from http://us.reachout.com/real-stories/story/loss

Psychological Blockages and Barriers. (2015). Retrieved from http://www.galamind.com/articles/psychological-barriers-and-block.aspx

Robins, Dale. (2015). The Power of Praise and Worship. Retrieved from http://www.victorious.org/praise.htm

What is the difference between praise and worship? Retrieved from http://www.gotquestions.org/difference-praise-worship.html

Wellman, Jack. (2014). Christian Crier. 7 Bible Verses About Patience with Commentary. Retrieved from http://www.patheos.com/blogs/christiancrier/2014/04/30/7-bible-verses-about-patience-with-commentary/

Lexicon Results. (2015). Retrieved from http://www.blbclassic.org/lang/Lexicon/Lexicon.cfm?Strongs=G5278&t=NASB&cscs=1Co

CPSIA information can be obtained
at www.ICGtesting.com
Printed in the USA
FSOW01n1017050915
10705FS